The New Face of Entrepreneurship

An Entrepreneurs Guide to Joy,
Passion and Profits in Business

By Michael Taylor

ISBN: 978-0-9969487-6-0 (Paperback Edition)

Library of Congress Control Number: 2018955326

Cover photos from unsplash.com

Contents

Foreword

Brandon Peele

The journey to genuine prosperity, an extraordinary purpose-driven life and a better world starts here.

Entrepreneurship is not hustle-or-die, @GaryVee struggle-porn. It's not the hyped-up glamour of "Billions" or "Shark Tank". It's one of the most profoundly sacred journeys you can take in this life. It's risking it all for the chance to have your life and career be a match for the majesty of your soul.

Michael Taylor has done all of us entrepreneurs a great service with this book, revealing the true face of entrepreneurship. Like all entrepreneurs, he has seen the highs, the lows, the in-betweens and the tap-outs ("Just give me a paycheck for Pete's sake"). What makes Michael unique and the path that he articulates in this book so powerful is that he is unafraid to explore the inner realms of being a human, knowing himself as a soul enfleshed by a body that walks the path of the entrepreneur.

Few entrepreneurs have done as much inner work as Michael Taylor. He has realized greater success and power by putting himself through the eye of the needle, through decades of spiritual practice and intense personal development work.

Baring it all in this book, you'll see a markedly different side of the entrepreneurial journey, one that is grounded in the scientifically, philosophically and spiritually defensible ideas of purpose and unity. You'll see that your higher or divine purpose is your path to realizing and expressing this unity, and the source of your entrepreneurial creativity, grit and resourcefulness. Without being grounded in this unity and your purpose, entrepreneurship would be insanity. Without it, who would take on that amount of risk and effort?

I've discovered in my work with entrepreneurs and leaders from all walks, that purpose is that origin story that connects your journey to the world, that fire that has you wake up, take your future into your own hands and innovate. This isn't just my experience, but the scientifically-validated path to success that I explore in my book, *Planet on Purpose.* Purpose-driven people experience higher levels of wealth, income, fulfillment and leadership effectiveness.

Further, when an organization is sourced by a higher or divine purpose, it can pivot more easily, evolve and the result is that it realizes growth rates that are three times higher than average. This purpose fuel also burns on Wall Street, as public purpose-driven organizations, like Johnson & Johnson and Canon, outperform the market 15:1.

That's just what your higher or divine purpose can do for the bottom line. It is also correlated with vitality (living 7 years longer), more loving relationships, better sex, overall contentment, and increased memory and cognition. In short, it makes you smarter, happier, sexier, wealthier and healthier. Who wouldn't want that?

To unleash your purpose-driven venture, start with Michael's book. Michael outlines the path and the key shifts in perspective necessary to create a life and business where you get it all - prosperity, connection, power, impact and creativity - through a deep connection to your own soul and the oneness of reality.

When you do, you will see the true face of entrepreneurship, know yourself as soul and your soul as one in the same as the world's. You'll know and feel what is yours to do in this world, a vital part of a global movement of soulful awakening.

On this journey, you'll step into a world that is unified in its diversity and connection to soul, one that stands as a beacon of hope in times beset by political dysfunction and the raging fires of social, economic and environmental injustice. You'll ignite the twin flames of soul and entrepreneurship to create an extraordinary life, a thriving business and a better world for future generations.

Brandon Peele
Author, *Planet on Purpose*
Berkeley, California
October 2018

Acknowledgements

First, foremost, and always, I must acknowledge the Infinite Intelligence that created and is still creating this amazing Universe that we live in. I use the term Source to try to define this energy and intelligence, but I recognize that words cannot come close to expressing the intimacy and trust I have developed over the years with Source. It is an internal knowing that I am connected to this power, which is greater than myself, and it is the source of my passion, drive, and creativity.

The closest I can get to expressing my gratitude is to say I love you more than love, and I am grateful for the connection I have with you. And so, I recognize that who I am is your gift to me and what I make of myself is my gift to you. I am certain that you are happy with my gifts to you because I am simply expressing all that you are through me.

And for this, I am truly grateful.

~ ~ ~

First of all, I must acknowledge Emmett McCoy (February 27, 1923 - January 7, 2012) for giving me the opportunity to climb the corporate ladder and become a manager for his multi-million dollar building materials company,

McCoy's Building Supply. Emmett gave an 18-year-old high school dropout the opportunity to manage one of his companies because he believed in me and recognized my potential.

He taught me countless lessons about running a company and being a great leader, and my business philosophy is based on the things I learned from him. One of his most powerful lessons was the KISS philosophy. *Keep It Simple Son* was his mantra and he applied this to all aspects of his business. He taught me to not get caught up in the trap of trying to impress others with fancy buildings and extravagant spending. Instead, focus on providing customers with the best possible products and the lowest possible price to make a profit and you will succeed. This principle works in life as well as business.

I am forever indebted to his generosity in sharing his wisdom with me and giving me the opportunity to learn how to be an entrepreneur who cares about their customers before caring about profits. Paradoxically, when you put your customers first, profits follow.

~ ~ ~

Next, I would like to acknowledge Reginald Lewis (December 7, 1942 – January 19, 1993) for being a role model that I try to emulate. Reginald was an inspiration because he was an entrepreneur who did not let race keep him from living his dream. As a man of color, I was drawn to his story because he was the first black man I was aware of who built a billion-dollar company. The book about his life is appropriately titled *Why Should White Guys Have All the Fun* and I have always felt the same way. One of my dreams is to build a billion-dollar business, and seeing Reginald pull it off lets me know that it is possible for me to do the same.

~ ~ ~

My current favorite entrepreneur is Peter Diamandis. He is a Greek American engineer, physician, and entrepreneur best known for being the founder and chairman of the X Prize Foundation, co-founder and executive chairman of Singularity University. He is a billionaire and author of two of my favorite business books, *Abundance* and *Bold*. He inspires me with his optimistic outlook, backed up by documented facts that the future is better than most people think. I really admire his commitment to entrepreneurs and his teachings and philosophies have deeply impacted how I think about being an entrepreneur. I refer to his teachings throughout this book and without question, his teachings have been the most impactful to me as an entrepreneur.

~ ~ ~

I would also like to thank Oprah Winfrey for being such an inspiration and influencer in my life. I remember one of the first times I watched her show, she was interviewing Gary Zukav and I was absolutely riveted to the television. I have always admired her for her willingness to go deeper into spiritual topics and her commitment to educating the masses about topics that mainstream media seldom showcased. As an entrepreneur, she inspires me with her business savvy and her ability to step out into unknown territory by launching her OWN network and creating her own personal platform based on her beliefs and values instead of what mainstream media generally promotes. Thank you, Oprah! I want you to know that I am setting an intention to appear on your Super Soul Sunday program, so be sure to leave a slot open for me.

~ ~ ~

I would also like to acknowledge my friend, mentor, coach, editor and all around really cool guy Brandon Peele. Brandon's book Planet on Purpose helped fuel my inner fire to make a positive impact on the world. It confirmed for me that each of us has a unique individual purpose and by discovering that purpose and then working with others who have also discovered their purpose, we can work collectively to heal the planet and unite humanity. As an irrepressible optimist, I deeply resonate with his work and I feel truly blessed to know him personally and to be a partner with him in creating a Planet on Purpose. You da man Brandon! I'm honored to work with you in creating a planet that works for everyone.

To each of these people, I say thank you. Thank you for leading the way and laying the foundation for entrepreneurs around the globe to follow in your footsteps. Because of you I am blazing my own trail and building a legacy that I know will make a major impact on the world.

~ ~ ~

Last but definitely not least, I'd like to acknowledge an

incredible group of people who believed in this book and me and were willing to support my crowdfunding campaign by purchasing some copies. I am eternally grateful for your support and I feel honored to place your name in this book.

So I'd like to send a shout out to: Arthur Johnson, Augie Bering, Bonnie Bering, Calvin Hayes, Charles Taylor, Katrina Taylor, Mike Taylor, David J. Dilger, Don Halverson, Fred Massey, James & Kelly Wyckoff, Jennifer Hutch, Kyle Barrow, Marcus Kirch, Michael Wilcov, Robert Hux, Robert Quint, Suzanne Pfardresher, Winnie Chatham, and Ronald Woliver.

Thank you to every one of you for your support and financial contribution.

Acknowledgements would not be complete if I didn't include my loving, supportive, and beautiful wife, Bedra. Thank you for your unconditional love and your belief in me. Your love is the fuel that empowers me to dream big and keep my commitment of making the world a better place. It is an absolute joy sharing life with you and I'm looking forward to the next chapter of our amazing life. You're the best!

Introduction

Contrary to negative mainstream media, I believe there has never been a better time to be alive on the planet than right now. The future is filled with infinite possibilities for anyone who is willing to put forth the effort and create the life of their dreams.

For some people, their dream is entrepreneurship, and this book is written specifically for them. Although there are hundreds of books written each year about starting and running a business, this book is a little different. The contents of this book do not focus on the *mechanics* of starting and running a business. The intention is to focus on the *Soul* of the business, which resides in the heart of the entrepreneur. To understand what I mean by the 'Soul of business' I will use the human body as a metaphor. The human body is comprised of multiple organs that each has individual functions. You have a brain, a liver, kidneys, eyes, a stomach and a heart. The heart is what gives a human being life, so it is arguably the most important organ in the body. As an entrepreneur, you are the heart that keeps your business alive.

Without question, it is important to understand the mechanics of building and running a business. An entrepreneur must learn how to create a business plan, as well as understand marketing and bookkeeping. They must know how to hire the right team and execute strategic plans to ensure their success. These are just a few of the "mechanics" of running a business, and although they are extremely important, they pale in comparison to the importance of understanding the Soul of the business.

I currently believe that entrepreneurship is actually evolving. Capitalism as we know it is changing, and for those of us who awaken to these changes we lay the foundation to create joy, passion, and profits in business. But instead of making profits our primary goal, entrepreneurs of tomorrow will make solving societal ills the primary focus and the reason for starting entrepreneurial ventures.

In some ways, entrepreneurship then becomes a spiritual practice and a path for ongoing personal development. The entrepreneur uses their enterprise as a means of self-expression and the business becomes an outlet for their creativity and their passions, and an opportunity to grow through overcoming obstacles. They are driven by a need to fully express who they are through their businesses, and they share their unique gifts and talents with the world through a particular product or service.

They see each social ill as a challenge that propels them to create solutions to the multiplicity of issues facing our world and they recognize that their products and services are part of the solution to those challenges.

It's been said that the easiest way to become a billionaire is to figure out a way to help a billion people. The New Face of Entrepreneurship is being driven by this idea. People who deeply care about the future and want to do their part in making the future better than the past drive it. It is driven by a deep urge to help heal the planet based on the idea there is only one race, which is the human race.

I happen to be an irrepressible optimist with a passion for the impossible because I truly believe that an entrepreneur can resolve every social ill facing our world today. There is no obstacle or challenge that cannot be overcome by an entrepreneur with vision, persistence, and perseverance. But most importantly, it takes deep passion and desire to want to make a difference in the world and I believe that can only come from the Soul of an entrepreneur.

I'm reminded of a quote by the late anthropologist, Margaret Meade:

> *"Never doubt that a small group of thoughtful, committed citizens can change the world; indeed, it's the only thing that ever has."*

This quote speaks directly to my belief that entrepreneurs can and will change the world.

So, you may be asking yourself, who is Michael Taylor, and why does he have the audacity to believe he can change the world? Simply put, I believe I can change the world because I believe every human being has a divine purpose and changing the world is part of my purpose.

I do not claim to be an expert or know-it-all; I have no college credentials or special training. What I do have is unwavering faith in my ability to create whatever my heart desires, and my desire is to build companies that change the world. I recognize that I definitely cannot do this alone, so I am enrolling people like you into my vision of a world that works for everyone, and I'm asking you to join me on my quest. The only requirement is for you to be open-minded and open-hearted enough to believe that we can change the world together. So, in the famous words of Napoleon Hill:

> *"Whatever the mind can conceive and believe it can achieve."*

I can see it, I believe it, and I can achieve it! What about you?

To prove my point, just remember that I had to overcome a multiplicity of challenges in order to be here writing these words. I've overcome being a high school dropout, divorce, bankruptcy, foreclosure, depression, and I was homeless for two years living out of a car. And yet I believed in my heart of hearts that I could overcome those challenges and here I am today, living my version of an extraordinary life as an entrepreneur, author, motivational speaker, radio, and TV host. It all began with me setting an intention in my mind and then working extremely hard to achieve what I believed.

For most of my life, I've been called a little crazy because of my optimism and belief in humanity. For those of you who may still believe I am a little crazy, I'd like to share a quote from one of my heroes and mentors, Steve Jobs:

Introduction

"Here's to the crazy ones, the misfits, the rebels, the troublemakers, the round pegs in the square holes... the ones who see things differently -- they're not fond of rules and they have no respect for the status quo... You can quote them, disagree with them, glorify or vilify them, but the only thing you can't do is ignore them because they change things... they push the human race forward, and while some may see them as the crazy ones, we see genius, because the ones who are crazy enough to think that they can change the world, are the ones who do."

Being one of the crazy ones means you are willing to follow your instincts in pursuit of something that only you can see. In most cases, it will appear to be irrational to others and people may call you crazy. People will say you're being unrealistic and maybe even lost touch with reality, but there is something inside you that says, "you can do this" and you must listen to that voice in your heart that knows you can.

As a former Atheist, there was a time when I was absolutely certain that God or a higher power didn't exist. I was convinced that believing in this power was irrational and there was no evidence that supported the idea that it was real. I held these beliefs very firmly for several years. I convinced myself that if science couldn't prove it, then it couldn't be real, so I embraced the idea that God was just an illusion.

After holding these beliefs for a few years, I then decided I would prove to myself that there was no such power in the universe, so I began researching and studying the major religions of the world. I read lots of books and spent countless hours speaking with people from different religions. I visited Buddhist temples, Jewish synagogues, Muslim mosques, Hindu temples, and a wide range of Christian houses of worship. As I listened to the leaders from a wide range of religions and studied their texts, I concluded that all religions essentially teach the same thing. They teach us that we have access to a Divine Intelligence that permeates the universe, and the goal of all religions is to help us connect to this Divine Intelligence. Because of my research and the amazing journey I went on to find my truth, I finally came to an understanding that works for me and I was able to develop an intimacy and a connection with this power and it has become the guiding force of my life. I do not try to convince people to believe what I believe, and I have the deepest respect for believers and non-believers alike. But I know with absolute certainty that there is definitely a power greater than myself that all human beings have access to, and when we connect to this power nothing is impossible.

If you have doubts about this power that is absolutely okay. I don't think you have to believe in it to become an entrepreneur. But if you truly want to become an NFE, then having a connection to this power is crucial.

There is a beautiful quote by the poet Rumi that I absolutely love. It says: "I searched for God and found only myself. I searched for myself and found only God."

I definitely do not want to come across as preachy. I remember how much that used to turn me off. So, if you're a little uncomfortable or even offended, I completely respect how you feel. Now it's up to you to decide if you want to continue, and the one thing I always preach is the power to choose. You get to choose what you believe, and you also get to choose whether or not you are willing to join me as one of the crazy ones.

If you're still reading, welcome to the Crazy Ones Club! I'm so glad you've joined us, and I look forward to sharing some insights that will guide you along your journey.

Michael

"Don't worry about being successful but work towards being significant and the success will naturally follow."

Oprah Winfrey

Chapter 1

What Is An Entrepreneur?

According to dictionary.com, an entrepreneur can be defined as: "a person who organizes and manages any enterprise, especially a business, usually with considerable initiative and risk." Using that definition, I'd like for you to recall the first person you think of when you hear the word *entrepreneur*.

Who comes to mind? Bill Gates? Elon Musk? Oprah Winfrey? Andrew Carnegie? Or maybe you thought of someone in your neighborhood who runs a grocery store, or a dry cleaners, or someone who sells items from the trunk of their car. Maybe you even thought about the kid who cuts grass for money or the young girl selling Girl Scout cookies or lemonade. Entrepreneurs come in all shapes and sizes, and there is literally no limit to what an entrepreneur can be or do.

Now I would like you to take a moment and try to imagine what it would be like to be an entrepreneur. In your mind, what do you picture? Do you envision someone who has lots of money, a big mansion, lots of fancy cars, maybe a private jet? What would the entrepreneur do on a daily basis? Would they be going to a hi-rise office building with lots of employees? Would they work 60-70 hours a week and be so stressed out that they really do not fully enjoy their success? How do you see the life of an entrepreneur?

The truth is, there are an infinite number of scenarios that could define and describe who an entrepreneur is and what they do. With that being said, I would like to share my definition of an entrepreneur.

An entrepreneur is simply *someone who receives compensation in exchange for a product or a service.* Contrary to the common definition, I do not believe you have to manage or organize a company or even make money to be an entrepreneur.

Let me explain what I mean. First, let's examine the word *compensation*, which can be defined as "the state of being compensated or rewarded in some way."

I believe there are three ways that you can be compensated as an entrepreneur:

1. Emotional
2. Spiritual
3. Financial

Overwhelmingly, the primary goal of most entrepreneurs would be to make money. When we think of entrepreneurship we generally think about financial compensation. The main reason we pursue money is because of the things we can buy which we think will bring us happiness and status (I'll talk more about this in an upcoming chapter).

Emotional compensation means we do something because it makes us feel good to do it. For example, I recently read a story about a woman named Debra Davis from San Diego, California. Debra drives around San Diego and serves homeless people free lunches. When she was asked why she spent her own money to feed homeless people her response was: "But you don't understand the joy I get from feeding people." Debra is an entrepreneur who receives emotional compensation in exchange for the food that she cooks and serves. She isn't interested in financial compensation because her reward is feeding people and making a difference in the world.

Spiritual compensation arises from a belief that we are fulfilling a divine purpose. For those who believe in a power greater than themselves, their purpose is to acknowledge that power by sharing their gifts and talents with the world. Their compensation comes from knowing they are fulfilling their unique mission in the world and they generally do not take credit for what they do because they recognize their higher power as the source of who they are.

The key as an entrepreneur is to prioritize which type of compensation you value the most. Is your primary goal to make money? Are you more interested in doing things that make you feel good? Or do you believe in a power that is greater than yourself and you are committed to fulfilling your divine purpose?

I believe you can have all three. To do so you must become an NFE, a New Face Entrepreneur.

As an NFE, I'd like to share how I prioritize the three types of compensation. For me, my first and most important form of compensation is spiritual. I believe there is an Infinite Intelligence that created and is still creating this amazing Universe we live in. This Intelligence goes by many names; God, Holy Spirit, Divine Energy, Chi, and a host of other names and labels. The name that is used to try to describe it is irrelevant. What's important is that we create an intimacy and connection with this Intelligence. For some people they create this connection through religion. Some may choose to follow Jesus or Buddha or Muhammad or Krishna, but ultimately these are just teachers who were sent here to guide you to your own understanding and connection to Infinite Intelligence.

The truth of the matter is you do not have to be religious or follow any religious dogma or doctrine to connect with and develop an intimacy with this Infinite Intelligence. All it takes is an open heart and an open mind that is open to new possibilities in your life and in your business.

As I understand it, this Infinite Intelligence is inherent in all things. My favorite metaphor for this Infinite Intelligence comes from my all-time favorite movie, Star Wars. In the movie this is described as The Force. Obi Wan Kenobi and the Jedi Knights have amazing powers in which they can read and influence other people's minds and move objects using only their minds through The Force. Obi Wan described The Force this way: "The Force is what gives a Jedi his power. It is an energy field created by all living things. It surrounds us, it penetrates us, and it binds the Galaxy together."

The Force is simply another name for God without any attachment to a particular religion. Although the story of Star Wars is based on fictional characters, I believe the movie is filled with Universal Truths and metaphors that we can apply to our everyday lives.

Because of my belief in the Infinite Intelligence that created the Universe I also believe that every human being has a divine purpose. It is our responsibility as human beings to discover our purpose and when we do everything else will fall into place. So, for me, this is the reason that spiritual compensation is my first priority.

My second priority is emotional compensation. As a writer, nothing compares to the feeling I get when someone tells me that my books have a positive impact on their lives. The joy I feel is nondescript and it's one of the primary reasons that I write. I love the feeling I get when I help someone improve their lives. As a speaker, I get the greatest high being on stage and sharing my message, watching and experiencing how the audience reacts while I'm speaking. There is an amazing energy I feel inside that literally lights me up and fills me with passion. This emotional compensation is another reason I work so hard to help people improve their lives. To repeat what Debra Davis so passionately stated: "You do not understand the joy I feel when I'm on stage. I love it so much I do it without the thought of compensation."

Last but not least, is *financial* compensation. There are some people who believe that you cannot be financially successful and spiritual at the same time. This is an erroneous belief that I want you to let go of. You *can* be rich and spiritual at the same time - there is absolutely nothing wrong with wanting to be extremely wealthy and have material things. The key is in prioritizing the three types of compensation. If you make money your highest priority, chances are you will never truly be happy. The old cliché is true: you can't buy happiness. On the other hand, if you make emotional compensation your highest priority then there is a very good chance you will end up being unhappy because you are not being compensated for the effort you're putting into your business. In other words, you'll probably end up broke. But when you open your heart to receive financial compensation as a reward for what you contribute to the world through your products or services then you become an NFE who is truly happy with their success.

~ ~ ~

As you read through this book, remember that an entrepreneur is simply someone who receives compensation in exchange for a product or service and they prioritize that compensation in the following order: Spiritual Compensation, Emotional Compensation, and Financial Compensation.

Universal Truths

If you are open to the idea that spiritual compensation should be your first priority, then it's important for you to understand a few basic Universal Truths. First, it's important to understand what it means to be a human being.

There are three realms to being human.

1. Your body
2. Your mind
3. Your spirit

I'll use the metaphor of a computer to explain how they all work together.

Your body is the physical computer. It is composed of electronic parts and circuits. It is the "hardware" or "body" and it comes with a variety of parts and components.

Your mind is the "software" that runs on the computer. It houses the programs that dictate what the computer can do.

Your spirit is the operating system in which your programs operate. Without an operating system, programs cannot work, and neither can the computer. The operating system is the soul of the computer and it uses the mind (software) to execute and carry out its functions.

The majority of people understand and identify with their physical bodies, which is the "computer". They believe they are their bodies and they are unaware of the programs that are actually running their lives. They refuse to understand that these programs cause them to act a certain way. They then accept societal labels and titles, which are just programs, to define who they are.

The amazing thing about a computer is you can change software and programming. To do so you must first access the operating system and then reprogram the software. Your spirit is that operating system, and to activate it you must first come to the understanding that you have access to it and you can change it. To do so you must embrace a Universal Truth that I learned from one of my mentors Dr. Wayne Dyer. Dr. Dyer proclaimed that we are not human beings having a spiritual experience, but we are actually *spiritual* beings having a *human* experience. In other words, we are the operating system, not the hardware or software of the computer.

If you can grasp this concept, then it should explain why receiving spiritual compensation first is so important. Since we are spiritual beings, these finite human bodies do not limit us. We are actually connected to the Infinite Intelligence (which is the Universal Operating System) that created the universe and we are therefore unlimited to what we can be, do, or have. When we are focused on spiritual compensation it deepens our connection to The Force and it provides us with the faith, patience, and perseverance to accomplish any goal.

In order to be an NFE it is absolutely imperative that you understand and identify with the idea that you are a spiritual being. To do so, you must be willing to challenge your beliefs and assumptions about the power that is greater than yourself, which I refer to as the Infinite Intelligence.

So, I'd like to ask you a few questions to help you become clearer on where you are regarding your spirituality. It is absolutely critical that you are completely honest with yourself in answering these questions. My intention is not to judge you or condemn you for your beliefs. No one will be able to hear or see your answers because I'm simply asking you to think. So, take a moment and ponder these questions. Remember, there are no right or wrong answers. There are only your answers, so answer honestly.

How would you describe the power greater than yourself?

Do you believe it exists?

Are you really clear about what you truly believe about this power, or have you simply accepted what your parents or culture has told you about it?

The reason I've shared these questions is because your beliefs about a power greater than yourself will definitely impact your life as an entrepreneur. Our belief about this power influences our actions and our outcomes whether we realize it or not.

For example, if you believe in a God that sees you as a sinner, and is an angry, judgmental white guy in the clouds, who takes notes of your life and waits for you to die so he can decide whether you get to go to heaven or hell, subconsciously that belief will have a negative impact on your life.

For example, when things aren't going well with your business you may rationalize it and say things like *I don't deserve it* or *it's God's will that I can't get my business started.* Subconsciously you will sabotage your business and then blame someone else for your apparent failure.

On the other hand, if you accept that there is a power greater than yourself that can only do one thing, which is to love you, then whenever you are faced with difficult challenges you can call on this power to give you faith and help you move through temporary setbacks.

Can you see the difference? One will empower you and the other will disempower you. Which will you choose?

It is important for you to come to your own conclusions about a higher power. It is a journey you must take on your own so that you become completely comfortable with your beliefs. Rest assured that your relationship with this power will either empower you or disempower you, so choose a path that's right for you and stick to it.

Leadership

If you're going to be an NFE you must accept the fact that you must become a leader. But a true leader isn't someone who says *follow me*, a true leader is someone who says, *I'll go first*. So, are you willing to go first and lead? Are you willing to bear the weight and responsibility of being responsible for the success or failure of your business? If that thought scares you a little that's okay. As a matter of fact, it should scare you just a bit.

It's been said that fear is the destroyer of dreams, so I want you to move through your fears and become the entrepreneur you know you're capable of becoming. In other words, *feel the fear and do it anyway*.

As an entrepreneur, you should be the heart and soul of

your business and the person everyone respects and looks up to for guidance and inspiration. As a leader, you must be smart enough to know when you need support in running your company. It means being willing to recognize the areas where you might be weak and be willing to step aside temporarily so someone else can take the lead. You must have confidence in yourself to do this, and it takes some vulnerability to let go of the reigns when someone else is leading, but that's the sign of true leadership.

Since you are the heart and soul of your business you must understand that your deepest values about business and life will be reflected in your company. If you are a person of honesty and integrity those values will filter down to everyone in the organization, and you have a good chance of building a successful company. On the other hand, if you are dishonest, egotistical, and arrogant, those qualities will be reflected in your organization and ultimately, I believe they will lead to your company's demise. There are lots of cases of entrepreneurs getting caught in fraudulent business practices, extramarital affairs, and unethical behavior which caused their business to fail, so make sure you don't become one of them.

I mentioned earlier about understanding Universal Truths and principles and one such principle is the law of Karma. Simply stated, Karma is the law of cause and effect. Put another way, whatever you put out into the universe comes back to you in a myriad of forms. For example, if you are filled with anger, resentment, and jealousy, whether you realize it or not those things will come back to you in some form. As an entrepreneur, it is important for you to understand how universal laws and Karma work.

A perfect example of this law and how it works in business is the current president of the United States (September 2018). He is the CEO of the largest, most powerful company in the world - the US Government. So, I'd like you to set aside any judgment you might have about him. It does not matter if you're a Republican or a Democratic. It doesn't matter if you hate him or you love him - this is a lesson in Karma, it isn't about politics.

As the CEO, his values and beliefs filter down through all levels of government. So, let's take a moment and look at the facts. This isn't fake news - these are all verifiable, substantiated facts. At the time of writing, five of his key advisors have been convicted of crimes and fired, while nineteen of his top advisors have resigned for various reasons. This has happened in less than two years on the job. This is an unprecedented level of corruption and turnover.

So, the question becomes, why? Is it because the White House is a terrible place to work? Well, I believe the answer lies with the President himself. As mentioned, Karma is simply a universal law that says what you put out comes back to you, and I will suggest that the reason the turnover and corruption is so high is because of the values the current President holds or does not hold.

When a person refuses to take responsibility for their actions and constantly blames everyone else for their problems, and in addition, they have an insatiable need for other people's approval, they are simply not very good leaders.

My hope is that you will use this as a learning experience on what not to do as an ethical leader in your endeavor.

As I mentioned, YOU are the heart and soul of your business. Your business will always reflect your deepest values and beliefs. It's important for you to understand that as a leader you actually give off an energetic frequency that will permeate throughout your organization. Remember Karma! What you put out there comes back to you.

~ ~ ~

So, you might be wondering, do you have what it takes to be an entrepreneur? The answer rests in what you believe: are entrepreneurs born or made? The short answer is both. A person can be born with a knack for business and while doing business discover their passion, or a person can be connected to their passion and realize that to express it they need to become an entrepreneur.

The deeper spiritual answer is that entrepreneurs are born with a divine purpose and it is up to them to discover and ultimately express that purpose.

I'd like to share my own story of becoming an entrepreneur, which is the reason I believe that being an entrepreneur is part of my divine purpose.

This is an excerpt from a book I wrote a couple of years ago titled: Adversity Is Your Greatest Ally.

~ ~ ~

The New Face of Entrepreneurship

When I was approximately 10-years-old I specifically remember a conversation I had with my grandfather about becoming an entrepreneur. Although I had no idea what that word meant at the time, I remember telling him that one day I was going to run my own company and become very rich.

As I sit here today writing about a conversation I had more than forty years ago, I still remember the conversation as though it were yesterday. I remember feeling the dirt between my toes and the sound of farm animals cackling in the background. I remember my grandfather's loving and supportive face as he encouraged me to pursue my dream and not let anything stop me. But most importantly, I remember the feeling of confidence and the intuitive knowing that I was destined to become an entrepreneur. In my heart and soul, I already knew what I wanted to do with my life, and I committed myself to live my dream and become a successful entrepreneur.

At the age of 14, I launched my first company, which put me on the fast track to fulfilling my destiny. By the time I was 17 I had built three different companies and I realized the entrepreneurial spirit was definitely encoded into my DNA.

During my junior year of high school, I enrolled in a special program that allowed a student to go to school for half a day and go to work the other half of the day and receive educational credits. I loved the program because it gave me the opportunity to gain first-hand experience in the business world while making money, and I took advantage of the situation and began learning everything I could about running a business.

One of our assignments was to create a presentation that we would share with the entire class and explain where we thought our lives would be 25 years into the future. I remember taking on the assignment and being so excited that I could barely sleep as I developed my presentation in my mind and on paper.

I already knew exactly what I wanted to be and do with my life, and my new assignment was going to give me an opportunity to share my dream with my class. As I was preparing my presentation, I did lots of research on wealthy businessmen. One of the men that I studied was a man named Napoleon Hill. He had written a book titled *Think & Grow Rich* and it was one of my favorites. One of the great lessons from the book was called "Definiteness of Purpose". I remember having trouble pronouncing the word, but I really grasped its true meaning. I had a deep knowing in my heart exactly what I wanted to do, and I had already begun laying the foundation for becoming an entrepreneur. In other words, I had a definiteness of purpose.

When the day came for my presentation I was ready. I had done my research, studied really hard, and practiced my presentation and now it was time to share it with my class (and ultimately with the world). When it was my turn to speak, I surprised the class by changing into a custom-made t-shirt that simply had 2% on it, without explaining what it meant.

I began my presentation by sharing the conversation that I had had with my grandfather about owning my own company when I was ten. I then shared how I started my first company at the age of fourteen and how I had already started three companies so far and I was still in high school. I talked about how passionate I was about being a businessman, and I even made a prediction that I would become a millionaire by the age of thirty and that I would be able to retire by the age of forty. I talked about being able to write multi-million dollar checks to charity because I believed that you should always give back once you make it to the top, and I was committed to using my money for the good of humanity. I talked about owning houses around the globe and being able to fly around in my private jet to visit them. I spoke about the high-rise building that my corporate offices would be located in and I talked about how I would create a corporate culture that created the best and brightest employees in the world.

I quoted some words of wisdom from some great business leaders and I explained to the class that I believed nothing was impossible, and that one day all my dreams would come true. When I finished, the entire class gave me a standing ovation and even the teacher said that he believed that I would accomplish all of my goals. As I was preparing to leave, I asked the students if they wanted to know what the 2% meant on my t-shirt. The majority of them said yes so I said: "The 2% t-shirt is a reminder that one day I will be in the top 2% of income earners in the country. It is a tool that I use to keep me focused and motivated."

Once again, the class began applauding and I walked off feeling more confident than ever.

This occurred back in 1977 when I was seventeen years old. And to this very day, it is still one of my most precious and proud moments. Although the entrepreneurial journey has had more ups and downs than I forecasted at 17, I can honestly say that I kept my promise to myself and followed my dream to become an entrepreneur. It was a dream that I became aware of at the tender age of ten and now here I am, some forty-something years later, and I realize that I listened to my heart and followed my dream.

~ ~ ~

I hope I've shed some light on what an entrepreneur is and how to be one. Remember, an entrepreneur is simply someone who receives compensation in exchange for a product or service and someone who prioritizes spiritual compensation, then emotional compensation, and finally financial compensation. With this frame of mind, you have the foundation for becoming a New Face Entrepreneur, a leader who makes a positive impact on the world.

Good luck!

"Success is not the key to happiness. Happiness is the key to success. If you love what you are doing, you will be successful."

Albert Schweitzer

Chapter 2

Do You Really Have What It Takes To Be An Entrepreneur?

If you're reading this book right now, the immediate answer to the question is yes, you definitely have what it takes to be an entrepreneur. Being an entrepreneur has nothing to do with age, race, religion, educational level, sexual orientation or social economic status. Truth be told, anyone can become an entrepreneur. Remember my definition of an entrepreneur is someone who receives compensation in exchange for a product or a service. Can you receive compensation for a product or service? If the answer is yes, then you too can become an entrepreneur.

However, being a successful entrepreneur is the real challenge and this should be your primary goal. So, remember, anyone can become an entrepreneur, but not everyone will be successful.

Traditionally, if you wanted to become an entrepreneur you would go to school to receive a business degree and once you received it you would then go out and secure a job with a big company to gain experience, eventually, you would come up with your own great idea and then you would launch your own company.

But those days are over. As a matter of fact, the old rules of starting a business no longer apply. So here is the really good news; there are no rules! That's right, there are really no rules when it comes to starting a business.

Of course, there are laws and regulations in running a business but when it comes to starting one the old rules do not apply.

So, let's take a look at some of the old rules.

Rule #1: You have to have a college degree to start a company.

Each year there are literally thousands of people who graduate from business schools around the globe. They are taught by some of the greatest minds in business and for all intents and purposes, you would think they would have an upper hand in creating companies. Our society has a rule that says someone with a degree is somehow more qualified to start and run a business than someone who does not have a degree. This rule definitely no longer applies.

Here's why: approximately 49% of all business owners do not have a college degree. You do not have to look very far to find successful entrepreneurs who never went or never completed their college degree. As a matter of fact, two of the richest entrepreneurs on the planet, Mark Zuckerberg (Facebook founder) and Bill Gates (Microsoft founder) never completed college.

The primary reason a college degree isn't necessary today

is because of the Internet. The Internet is the great equalizer for entrepreneurs. Because of the Internet, every entrepreneur now has instant access to an infinite amount of information and education that used to only be available through prestigious business schools. Did you know you can now take free courses from some of the most accredited universities in the world online? For free! Imagine being able to learn from professors and educators in the comfort of your own home at no cost to you! Did I mention it's FREE! Don't believe me? Check out iTunes U in the App Store to see for yourself.

In addition to that resource, there are lots of others for little or no cost that will give you all the education you need to start and run a business. There are companies like YouTube, Udemy, Coursera, and EDX that give you direct access to everything you need to start and run your business successfully. So, the old rule of needing a degree to start and run a company is no longer applicable. All it takes is willingness to learn and commitment to apply what you learn to starting and running your business.

Rule #2: Location, Location, Location

Just 25 years ago one of the most important keys to a successful business was location. Brick and mortar stores were the key to building successful companies. The better the location, the more traffic you received and the more money you would make. In case you haven't noticed, retail stores have been steadily declining over the past several years as more and more companies shift their focus to online shoppers. Companies now recognize that the future of business is shifting to convenience and ease for the younger generation, who were raised in the culture of emerging online technologies.

This rule has been completely abolished because of the Internet and technology. You are no longer restricted by physical and geographical locations. Anyone can now reach customers around the globe and there is literally no limitation to where you can find customers for your product or service.

Rule #3: It takes a lot of capital to start a business

One of the most challenging aspects of starting a business is raising capital. Although this is still an obstacle, the barriers to securing funding have dropped significantly. First of all, there are more alternative funding sources than ever before (I'll go into more detail on this in an upcoming chapter). But more importantly, the cost of starting a business has dropped considerably over the past decade or so. For example, back in 1995, I launched a business and I needed to hire a graphic designer to create a cartoon mascot for my company. At the time a graphic artist charged between 200 and 500 dollars per hour. After doing lots of research (mostly by going through the phone book and contacting design firms) I narrowed down my search to two firms based on their experience and their price. I decided on one of the firms and the total cost of the design job was approximately three thousand dollars. Today, I can have that same job done with a lot more options for around five hundred dollars. This is because of the abundance of freelancer design companies that allow you to post your jobs on their websites and freelance designers bid on your projects.

Another advantage entrepreneurs have today is access to information and technology that lowers the cost of business services considerably. For example, I save myself thousands of dollars per year by willing to learn how to do things myself rather than hire someone to do them. I taught myself how to build websites and how to shoot and edit video. I taught myself how to launch a podcast and host an online radio show. I learned how to self-publish my books and set up worldwide distribution channels. And I learned how to find people to do things I can't do, like bookkeeping, copywriting, and marketing.

Although it may be difficult to secure funding for your business, rest assured that there has never been a better time to start than right now, and if you're committed enough you will find a way.

So, let's review those 3 'rules' one more time:

1. You have to have a college degree to start a company
2. Location, Location, Location
3. It takes lots of capital to start a business

You must accept the fact that these rules no longer apply and the only thing that can keep you from starting a business is yourself. There are no rules, and the only limitations you have are those that exist in your mind.

Got it? Good! Let's move on!

Now that you know you have what it takes to be an entrepreneur, I'm going to share with you the key to your success. This is something that isn't taught in business school. This lesson comes from playing the game of life and learning from some of the great entrepreneurs of the past and present. This lesson comes from my own 25-year journey of research and self-discovery and it is the foundation of my success.

Would you like to know what it is? Would you like to know the one thing that will ensure your success, not only in business but also in every area of your life?

The key to ensuring your success as an entrepreneur and as a human being is to discover who you really are! Knowing who you really are means knowing your unique gifts and talents and how you can use them to change the world. It means understanding what lights you up from the inside and drives you to do whatever is necessary to reach your fullest potential. It means recognizing the oneness of humanity and how everything is connected and therefore you intuitively know that there is no separation between you and other human beings. It means embracing your divinity and coming to the understanding that you are a divine manifestation of the Infinite Intelligence that created and is still creating this amazing Universe that we live in.

That's it! Knowing who you really are is the key that guarantees success. Unfortunately, very few people are willing to wake up to and discover who they really are. Most people would rather hide behind socially constructed masks and pretend to be something they really aren't. Too many times they get caught up in titles and labels and they get stuck in these societally generated boxes and conform to the status quo.

The key to success is to break free from these societal cages and discover your true authentic self. To do this you will have to come to the understanding that you are not a human being having a spiritual experience - you are a spiritual being having a human experience.

If you are willing to accept this idea and are committed to discovering who you truly are, then I want to share some insights I wrote in one of my previous books. These insights will support you in waking up to your authentic self and my hope is it will change your perception of yourself in a positive way.

As mentioned in the previous chapter, every major religion points to the idea that you have a spark of divinity within you. You have direct access to the Infinite Intelligence that created, and is still creating, this amazing Universe and it is up to you to tap into this divinity.

I want to share a quote by Dr. Richard Bartlett:

> *"You are more than your thoughts, your body, or your feelings. You are a swirling vortex of limitless potential who is here to shake things up and create something new that the Universe has never seen."*

As you read the quote, what thoughts came to mind? How did you feel after reading it? Did you feel excited? Scared? Confused? Uncertain? What if the quote is true? What if I told you that you are an unlimited being with infinite potential? Would you believe me?

Unfortunately, most people wouldn't. But the fact that you are reading this book right now tells me that you are not "most people". If you are the type of person who reads a book like this, that tells me that you are open-minded, curious, and willing to learn and grow, and therefore it's quite possible that you believe the quote. As a matter of fact, you've probably already agreed with it and are now ready to create something new that the Universe has never seen - so let's just jump right in and get started.

The truth is, there's an overwhelming majority of people who do not believe the quote. They will accept societally driven labels that define who they are without ever asking themselves deeper questions like, "who am I" and "why am I here?" This chapter is designed to give you some insights on possibly answering those two questions for you. Are you ready to answer those questions for yourself?

If you ask most people who they are, they will usually respond with answers such as their name, whether they have a family, what they do for a living, if they are a democrat or republican, an African American, Asian, Latino or Caucasian, a Christian or a Muslim (or are part of a host of other religions), an American or an immigrant - the list of labels goes on and on. But if you think really deeply about this, these are just titles and labels that we use to try to define who we are. To prove my point, I want you to do a simple test. Walk up to a mirror and ask yourself what you see. Do you see a Republican? A Christian? A husband? A manager?

The answer is that you see a human being. The mirror can't

lie, it can only reflect that which is placed in front of it. All the titles and labels that you use to define yourself isn't who you are; they are simply titles, labels, and beliefs that you have accepted to define yourself. For example, have you ever known someone who used to be a Republican, but then became a Democrat? Or someone who was a Christian, who then became a Muslim? Or maybe someone who was pro-life, then became pro-choice? If they looked in the mirror as a Republican and then became a Democrat what would they see in the mirror? They would see a human being, not a label. Labels are really just beliefs. You are not a label. You are a human being with different beliefs, and although your beliefs may change, you will not.

What you see in the mirror is what you truly are, but it goes a lot deeper than that. *What* you are, is not necessarily *who* you are.

Let me explain in more detail.

What you are is a human being with flesh and bones. This is an undisputable fact. But *who* you are is the divine being that resides within the flesh and bones. Here is another way to look at it - if I stand in front of a mirror and look at myself, I notice that I'm wearing a shirt. So, if I say that it is "my" shirt, who owns it? I do - it is "my" shirt. Now, I continue to look in the mirror and notice my body.

Who is the "me" that owns the body? If this is "my" body, who am I? I would like to suggest that the "me" that owns the body is actually my spirit. To repeat that essential phrase, *you are not actually a human being having a spiritual experience - you are a spiritual being having a*

35

human experience, and your body is just like the suit of clothes that you are wearing.

If you can wrap your mind around this idea, then the original quote that I began this chapter with should make more sense to you. The quote said, *"You are a swirling vortex of limitless potential who is here to shake things up and create something new that the Universe has never seen."* Which simply means that you are a divine spiritual being expressing yourself through human form. You have unique gifts and talents that must be shared with the world if you truly want to live a rewarding and fulfilling life.

If you're familiar with the story of Jesus, you may remember that he stated, *"These things and even greater things you shall do also."* So what *things* was he talking about? According to the story, he healed the sick, read minds, predicted the future, and even raised people from the dead. So, based on his own admission, we are all capable of doing all of those things. And yet very few people are willing to accept this as a possibility. Why? Because most people are unwilling to embrace their divinity. Most people can't accept that they are "swirling vortexes of limitless potential" who came here to "shake things up."

I fervently believe that this was Jesus' primary message. That we all have a divine spark of the Infinite Intelligence that created the Universe within us, and if we learn to access this spark nothing is impossible.

So, what do you think? Do you believe this? Can you accept that you are much more than your physical body? Can you embrace the idea that you are a divine spiritual being with unlimited potential who is here to shake things up?

Since you're still reading this book that means you're ready to dive deep into who you really are! So, let's begin with understanding your divine makeup.

As mentioned earlier, you are actually a three-part being which can be described as body, mind, and spirit. You are a spirit, which is housed in a body that has a mind. Your body is like the clothes you are wearing, and your mind is like a tool that you use to help make conscious decisions and to learn new things. They all work in harmony.

As a spiritual being, you have an infinite capacity for learning and creativity. There are absolutely no limits to the amount of things you can learn and create. You are only limited by your imagination, and even your imagination is unlimited.

So, let's break down the three parts of your being.

Let's begin with your mind.

It's important that you understand what your mind is and how it works if you truly want to discover who you really are. I'll begin by saying that the mind and the brain are not really the same thing. Your brain is the organ that serves as the center of your nervous system and is responsible for cognitive thinking and memory. In my opinion, it is the most amazing organ in your body and it works just like a muscle - the more you use it, the stronger it gets.

The mind, however, is separate and distinct from the brain,

although they work together. It is almost impossible to truly define the mind. Scientists have been trying to define it in scientific terms for millennia, but unfortunately, there has never been a consensus on exactly what the mind is. Rather than try to argue and define it, I will simply share a definition that I truly resonate with, and it is this definition I will use to explain what I believe the mind does and how it works.

The mind is "*the element of a person that enables them to be aware of the world and their experiences, to think, and to feel; the faculty of consciousness and thought.*"

I really like the last part of this definition; *the faculty of consciousness and thought.*

According to Dr. Bruce Lipton, author of the amazing book *The Biology of Belief,* the mind actually has two parts: the conscious mind and the subconscious mind. A great metaphor to explain how it works is an iceberg. If you look at an iceberg you will only see a small portion of it above the water, but did you know that in some cases 90% of the iceberg is actually below the surface? This is how the mind works. The top 10% is your conscious mind and the lower 90% is your subconscious mind. What is really fascinating is that the subconscious mind is actually 1,000 times more powerful than the conscious mind when it comes to influencing your behavior.

Dr. Lipton explained it this way;

When we are born, we are completely conscious of all the external stimuli that we interact with. As children we process primarily through our feelings without judgment or thought about the situation. In other words, we use our hearts, not our minds, to interpret everything around us. Our feelings become the guidepost of our experiences.

During the first 7-10 years of our lives, our subconscious mind works like a video recorder. It simply records all the external events in our lives, and then it begins associating feelings, memories, and beliefs with those events. As we grow older, we begin to form subconscious beliefs about everything we come into contact with. As we form these beliefs we then begin making assumptions about who we are and how we fit into the world. Our prerecorded tapes become our subconscious beliefs about ourselves, and everything we think and do are then filtered through, and influenced by, these prerecorded tapes.

So, take a moment to think about your own childhood, especially between when you were born and when you turned seven. What do you remember? Do you remember growing up in a loving, caring home, or was it one filled with violence and dysfunction?

Whether you realize it or not, your childhood has a strong impact on your behavior, even as an adult. If you remember being loved and nurtured as a child, the chances are your subconscious mind is filled with positive beliefs about yourself. In other words, your prerecorded tapes are positive, which in most cases means you will feel good about yourself and have a positive attitude about life. On the other hand, if you remember pain and misery growing up, there is a good chance that your prerecorded tapes about yourself may be negative, which in turn may cause you to create a negative outlook on life.

You can look at the subconscious mind as a big memory bank that stores your beliefs, memories, and life experiences. All your thoughts are instantly processed through your subconscious beliefs. Look at it this way - once your subconscious tapes are programmed during your childhood every thought and action you have as an adult will be based on the programming you experienced growing up.

I'd like to take this time to share an example from my own life.

I was separated from my mom at the age of six, where I then created a subconscious belief that the people who love you will always leave you. As an adult that may sound irrational but as a six-year-old my mother meant the world to me, and her leaving me was devastating and emotionally traumatizing.

As a result of this event, I created a subconscious belief that there was something wrong with me that caused my mother to leave. The primary belief I created was that I was unlovable. In order to not feel the shame and abandonment I experienced when my mother left, I created a subconscious strategy that I thought would keep me from feeling pain, and also to keep the people in my life from leaving.

That strategy was for me to become a super nice guy in the hopes of keeping people around who I cared about. By becoming a super nice guy, I put other people's emotional and psychological needs ahead of my own, and I was constantly trying to take care of others before taking care of myself. This is called *co-dependency*, and it was the reason I struggled with relationships as a young adult.

I didn't realize it as I was growing up, but that single event laid the foundation of how I interacted in all of my relationships as an adult. My subconscious beliefs about myself actually sabotaged my relationships.

I would enter into a relationship where I would be the super nice guy. I would do all the right things that a woman would want in a relationship. I was attentive and respectful, and I had no problems showing affection. I had a great sense of humor and definitely believed in monogamy. On the surface, I appeared to be the perfect guy, but unfortunately, my subconscious beliefs about not being good enough and the deep-seated fear of abandonment kept me from being truly authentic in relationships, which kept me from experiencing true intimacy. No matter how much a woman loved me, that deep-rooted fear I had convinced me that something was wrong with me, which led to the fear that eventually the women in my life would leave.

Based on this subconscious fear, what do you think happened in my relationships? Of course, the women in my life would leave. I created an amazing pattern in all of my relationships, especially after my divorce. I would enter into a relationship and it would last two to three weeks, and then the woman would end up saying that they "cared too much" about me to stay in the relationship.

At the time it made absolutely no sense to me that women would say that. How could you care about someone, but at the same time leave them? After some deep self-introspection and emotional healing, I was able to recognize how my subconscious beliefs had been sabotaging my relationships, and I figured out how to break the pattern.

The point I'm trying to make is how powerful the subconscious mind really is. Remember, the subconscious mind is separate and distinct from your brain - it is the faculty of consciousness and thought.

On the other hand, you have your conscious mind, which could be referred to as your "intellect". The conscious mind is where you store information that you have learned through rigorous study and learning. When you go to school and learn facts you are using your conscious mind. When you calculate and figure out solutions to most problems you are also using your conscious mind, but remember what I said about the subconscious mind being 1,000 times more powerful than the conscious mind?

Here is an example of how this works:

Imagine you know someone who has a PhD in astrophysics. This person is obviously extremely intelligent and has a highly developed conscious mind. But imagine, too, that this person has difficulty creating healthy relationships. No matter what they do, they always experience difficulty in relationships. Why do you think this is? They are obviously very smart, and yet they can't figure out how to make relationships work. Why is that?

Well, it's actually pretty simple. On a conscious level, they can read a book about relationships and explain to you intellectually how relationships work - activities which use the conscious mind. But their subconscious is 1,000 times more powerful than their conscious mind, so when they enter into a relationship the subconscious beliefs they have about themselves will always override the conscious mind. No matter how many books they read or how smart they are, if they have deeply rooted negative subconscious beliefs about themselves they will never be able to create healthy relationships.

This is why it is so important to understand how the mind works. No matter how much we may learn on a conscious level, if we aren't willing to look at our subconscious beliefs we can never truly change our lives. We each have deeply held subconscious beliefs about a wide variety of things and until we become willing to change these subconscious beliefs we will not be able to overcome our subconscious conditioning.

Let's take a look at some subconscious beliefs that may be sabotaging your life right now.

Are you currently struggling financially and can't figure out why? Well, there is a very good chance that your subconscious beliefs are actually keeping you from being financially secure. If you grew up hearing that money was the root of all evil or that rich people were stuck up and selfish then you may have subconscious beliefs keeping you from making a lot of money, because your subconscious belief might be that money is "bad".

If you're a man and you struggle with relationships, you may have subconscious beliefs that say women only want you for your money or women can't be trusted. This belief will eventually sabotage any new relationship you enter. If you're a woman and struggle with relationships, then it's quite possible that you have subconscious beliefs that say all men are dogs and only want sex. Therefore, this belief will keep you from creating true intimacy with men because of your lack of trust.

If you happen to be religious, you may have subconscious beliefs that you are a sinner and there is nothing you can do except repent for your sins and hope that God forgives you for being a sinner.

No matter what subconscious beliefs you have you must understand that it is those beliefs that are actually the cause of most of the pain, suffering, and lack of experience you have in life.

To sum it up, your subconscious beliefs create your reality, so if you aren't happy with any area of your life right now I can assure you the main reason is that you have some subconscious belief causing you pain and misery.

It is absolutely imperative that you begin examining your deeply held subconscious beliefs if you truly want to change but rest assured that it *is* possible for you to do so.

Now that you have a deeper understanding of how the subconscious mind works, here's the really good news - when you realize just how powerful the mind really is, you can use it to create anything you want in life.

Have you ever heard this quote: "Whatever the mind can conceive, you can achieve, if you really believe"?

Do you believe it? Is it really possible?

I believe the answer is "yes" and now I would like to share how and why this is possible. So, let's go back to the definition I posted earlier: The mind is *"the element of a person that enables them to be aware of the world and their experiences, to think, and to feel; the faculty of consciousness and thought."*

I would like you to focus on *"the faculty of consciousness and thought."*

Here is another way to look at it. Try to imagine there is a Divine Intelligence that permeates the Universe. This Intelligence is actually the Source of all things. It is inherent in all things. It is what keeps the planets aligned and what causes a seed to grow into a flower. It is the same intelligence that causes a bone to heal and the earth to orbit the sun.

There are lots of different names for this Source, but the name does not matter. You can call it God, The Creator, Yahweh, Jehovah, Great Spirit, The Universe, or any other name, but what is most important is that you believe and trust that it is available to you (throughout this book I will simply refer to it as The Source). You do not have to believe in any particular religion or dogma to have access to it, you must simply open your heart and your mind to the truth that it exists. If you accept this truth, then you must accept that your mind is actually connected to The Source. Your mind is like a conduit through which The Source allows divine intelligence to flow to you and through you.

Now you must remember what I said at the beginning of this chapter. **The mind and the brain are not the same thing.** The brain can only process information that you have provided it. The brain is not creative - it is not the source of imagination, creativity, or divine ideas. The brain is also not the source of inspiration or insight - these are all functions of the mind, which can also be referred to as the heart, or the center of your being.

Author and spiritual teacher Iyanla Vanzant said:

> *"The mind is a powerful, creative energy. Everything we think, do and feel begins in the mind. For this reason, we have to address the thoughts, beliefs, judgments, learnings, and perceptions that we hold in our minds."*

The reason the quote "whatever the mind can conceive you can achieve" is true, is because The Source of all things is purely creative, and it needs you to co-create with it. So, when your mind conceives a divine idea from The Source, which is all-powerful and limitless, you can accomplish it if you're willing to work hand-in-hand with The Source and put forth a whole lot of effort to bring it to fruition.

One of my favorite spiritual teachers is Deepak Chopra. He shared a very powerful quote that really speaks to this truth. He said: "Inherent in every intention and desire are the mechanics for its fulfillment." Put another way, The Source will not give you an idea that you can't accomplish. The Source knows exactly what you're capable of and will therefore only give you divine ideas that are attainable for you. You wouldn't even have the idea in the first place if you weren't capable of accomplishing it.

As I mentioned previously, the mind is the source of imagination, and therefore it is the key to creating anything you want in life. Let me share a brief story with you to validate my point.

During the darkest period of my life, I was deeply depressed and unsure of how I was ever going to get my life back on track. At the time I had no money, no job, no relationship, and no material possessions, and things seemed pretty hopeless. But the one thing I did have was my imagination, and I began to use it to help me change my situation. Despite that I had absolutely nothing, I began imagining my life getting better. Instead of focusing on all the things I didn't have, I focused my attention on what I *did* have. I would begin each day counting my blessings for everything that I had, such as my health, my ability to learn, my positive attitude, a few close friends, children who loved me, and the fact that I was even alive.

I began envisioning what my life would be like once I got back on my feet, and I somehow knew that eventually, I would. As I continued to focus on the things I did have and on the future I wanted to create, things slowly started to change for me. Eventually I found a job, then I purchased a car, and finally, I was able to get my own apartment. Although this took a couple of years, my point is that I used my imagination to see the things I wanted, and then I worked really hard to get them. It all began in my mind. I had to be willing to use my mind and imagination first before I could create the things I wanted.

In retrospect, I can now see how The Source was actually the source of all of the ideas I used to put my life back together. It was The Source that would provide me with ideas on where to look for employment and gave me the inspiration to remain positive even when I had nothing. It was The Source that gave me the strength and courage to move through all of my life's challenges without giving up and falling victim to despair. It was The Source that encouraged me and helped me to focus on my ultimate destiny, and it didn't allow me to quit.

Even through those difficult times, I held on to my dreams of one day being a successful entrepreneur, writer, and speaker. I had no evidence that I could do these things, I only had the belief and faith that I could. Belief and faith originate in the mind, and I now recognize that each of these originate from The Source.

And now here I am, some twenty-five plus years later doing exactly what I imagined I would be doing. All because I chose to believe that whatever the mind can conceive, you can achieve.

It's important that you understand I am no different than

you are. I am a divine spiritual being with direct access to The Source, and so are you. There is nothing you cannot accomplish if you choose to access your divinity, but it is up to you to go a little deeper and figure out what negative subconscious beliefs you may have about yourself and change them. It is your responsibility to learn more about your mind and begin using it to create the life you deserve. This is simply an overview of how your mind works. I simply want you to accept and understand that your mind is the most important aspect of your humanity. Don't take it for granted. Use it to create the life you were born to live. It is your greatest gift from The Source.

Now, let's talk about your body.

It is my belief that the most amazing thing on this planet is the human body. I do not believe there is anything more miraculous. Although most people take their bodies for granted I believe it is the greatest gift The Source has provided us. I mentioned earlier that the body is simply a suit of clothing that your spirit wears, so I must admit The Source knew exactly what it was doing when it created the human body.

Of course, everyone is aware of their own physical body, but did you know you also have an emotional or energetic body?

If you accept the fact that you are a spiritual being then it makes it easier to grasp how the emotional/energetic body works.

Think of it this way:

Imagine you have an opening in the top of your skull and there is a pipe going from the top of your skull to the bottom of your belly. This pipe flows with energy that comes directly from The Source - this energy is your life force and permeates your entire being. When you are born the pipe is completely open and it allows Source energy to flow through you easily. This energy causes you to feel alive and connected to life. This energy is then converted into feelings, which is the spirit's way of communicating with the body. There are primarily four energies that move throughout the energetic body: joy, anger, sadness, and fear.

As a child, whenever you experienced one of these feelings you acted appropriately and expressed the feeling through an emotion. For example, if you felt sad you would cry; if you felt angry you would scream or lash out; if you felt joy you would smile and laugh, and if you felt fear you would close off or retreat. As long as you expressed the feeling appropriately, then the energetic pipe stayed open and clear and your life force energy continues to flow through you.

As you grow older, your parents or family members begin conditioning you to believe that expressing these emotions was wrong, so what happens is you begin to repress and suppress your feelings, and each time you do you begin to create little energy blocks in the pipe. It's like building up plaque in your arteries. The more you suppress your feelings, the more the energetic pipe clogs up, and before you know it the pipe is completely closed, and you are cut off from your life force. When this happens, you lose your sense of aliveness, because the divine flow of energy has been cut off. Once the flow of energy has been cut off and we have been disconnected from The Source we then learn to process everything through our conscious mind or intellect, and we become very rational and analytical. In other words, we try to rely on our brains instead of our minds and hearts.

The bad news is the energetic body works like the subconscious mind. We may not be aware of it, but our repressed emotions cause us to act out irrationally sometimes because we are completely unconscious of the pain we may be carrying. Here is a good example: Have you ever met someone or known someone who is always angry? No matter what is going on, this person is angry and negative, and they usually aren't that pleasant to be around. They get angry and upset at the slightest provocation, and no matter what you say or do they will have a negative response to just about everything. Do you know anyone like that? Are *you* like that?

Why do you think this person acts this way? It's because they have trapped emotional energy in their emotional body, and until they learn how to release it they will always act out of anger.

On the flip side of that, maybe you know someone who always pretends to be happy. They are the "people pleasing" types who always seek approval and they pretend everything is always okay. The only emotion they express is happiness, but unfortunately, they are completely sad and emotionally bankrupt inside. A person like this usually has trapped anger, fear, or sadness in their emotional bodies, and rather than feel these emotions they hide behind being happy all of the time.

When we have repressed or suppressed emotions they can sabotage all areas of our lives. As long as we feel and release our feelings appropriately the life force can move through us, but as we shut down the flow we create a disconnection from The Source and it leads to all sorts of problems in our lives.

It's important that you take care of both of your bodies - your physical body and your emotional one. You take care of the physical body by eating the right foods and exercising and you take care of the emotional body by investing in some emotional healing work that allows you to release any repressed energy trapped in your emotional body.

Now that you have a better understanding of how the mind and the body work together it's time to fully understand who you really are.

Every major religion promotes a very simple and profound truth. There is a Source through which all things are created. It does not matter which religion you follow, as long as you accept this simple fact. This Source is the Divine Intelligence that created and is still creating the Universe, and you have unlimited access to this Source. As a human being, you are a divine expression of this Source, which means that you can co-create anything your heart desires with this Source.

Think of it this way - if you look at the ocean, you will see a powerful, beautiful, and seemingly infinite body of water. If you walk up to the ocean and scoop up a small cup of it, what you will have in the cup is ocean. But the cup of ocean could never be the ocean in its totality, so therefore it is a divine expression of the ocean. This expression is no different than the ocean; as a matter of fact, it contains all of the same qualities, characteristics, and attributes of the ocean. In fact, it is the ocean in an individualized expression. As long as the *expression* of the ocean stays connected to the ocean it will thrive and express exactly the way the ocean does. But if the ocean in the cup is separated from the ocean, eventually it will dry up and no longer exist as that unique expression.

The Source is just like the ocean. You are an individual expression of the Source. You have all the same qualities, characteristics, and attributes as the Source. You are no different than The Source. As long as you stay connected to The Source you can co-create with it - and since The Source is infinite so are you.

Do not buy into societal labels and constructs that will convince you there is something wrong with you. Disregard all labels and titles and come to the understanding that you are a divine spiritual being with unlimited potential, and the only thing keeping you from accomplishing anything is yourself. This includes letting go of your attachment of your ethnic identity. You should definitely be proud of your ethnic heritage, whatever it may be, but you must understand your spiritual nature has nothing to do with skin color or nationality. The Source transcends race and therefore so do you if you choose to accept who and what you truly are.

Titles and labels will only hold you back but accepting the truth of your being will definitely set you free. Remember you are a three-part being - Spirit, Mind, and Body - connected to The Source, and you can, therefore, co-create anything your heart desires.

Here is a metaphor about snowflakes I would like you to think about:

If you look at snowflakes falling from the sky it appears they're all the same. They all have the same color, texture, and smell. They're all composed of the same stuff, and they all come from the same source. But if you look under a microscope every snowflake is completely different. No two snowflakes are alike. Just imagine – out of the billions of snowflakes that fall from the sky, none of them are the same.

The truth is, you are just like the snowflake. Out of the 7 billion human beings on the planet, there is only one you. When it comes to human beings, The Source never replicates itself. You are a divine, unique individual expression of The Source, and it is your responsibility to accept this fact.

Your job is to come to this understanding and to recognize that you have unlimited potential and you have been given some unique gifts and talents that are yours alone - and your job is to share them with the world. This is the reason the quote I shared at the beginning of this chapter is so important. It states a divine truth, and I hope you will take it to heart and accept it as *your* truth.

So, I would like for you to reread the quote and embrace it and accept the truth it shares:

> *"You are more than your thoughts, your body, or your feelings. You are a swirling vortex of limitless potential who is here to shake things up and create something new that the Universe has never seen."*

In the case of an entrepreneur, the something new the Universe has never seen will be a company you create to "leave a dent in the Universe" as Steve Jobs put it.

So, take the time to truly know yourself. Invest in your own potential. Find the things that light you up and make you want to get out of the bed each morning with joy, excitement and expectancy. Learn to fall in love with yourself and your life and express your heart's desires in ways that make you happy and proud. Become an NFE and make a positive impact on the world.

I'd like to close this chapter with a question by Dr. Ibram Kendi. In a powerful commencement speech, he posed the question: Are You an Intellectual?

Here is the transcript of part of that speech. Be sure to take the time and read it thoroughly and slowly, and then answer the question for yourself.

~ ~ ~

I want to talk to you about what is next for your mind. The point of my address is to ask you a very simple question. Are you an intellectual?

I'm asking this question because you need to know that having a doctorate does not make you an intellectual. Becoming a professor does not make you an intellectual. Working in a research lab does not make you an intellectual. Just like there are MDs who are not healers. Just like there are reverends who are not about God.

Do not become that person.

No doctorate degree is required to join the intellectual academy. This is an inclusive academy with all types of people coming from all types of backgrounds. There are people with only a GED, there are incarcerated people, there are homeless people in this intellectual academy. There are poor people in this intellectual academy.

So, when I say intellectual, I'm not referring to someone who knows a wealth of information. All of you, I'm sure, know a lot. I do not measure a person's intellect based on how much a person knows. How much you know has no bearing on how much you are an intellectual.

I defined, and many others define an intellectual as someone with a tremendous desire to know. Intellectuals have a tremendous capacity to change their minds on matters, to self-reflect, to self-critique. Intellectuals are only governed by one special interest. And that special interest is rarely self-serving. And that special interest is finding and revealing the truth.

How many of you have a tremendous desire to know? How many of your minds are wide open to new ideas? How many of you are searching for ideas that challenge how you see the world? How many of you are willing to look differently at the world with the blink of new evidence? How many of you are critiquing your own ideas as intensely as you critique the ideas of others?

Intellectuals are a nomadic people—constantly changing their conceptual location, constantly in search of a better conceptual space. You know we have workout warriors of the body. Those who pump iron to break down old muscles to allow newer and bigger and better muscles to grow in their place. Well, intellectuals are workout warriors of the mind; regularly breaking down old ideas to allow new ideas and bigger ideas and better ideas to grow in their place.

Are you an intellectual?

"I believe that the free enterprise system is the greatest engine of prosperity the world's ever known."

Barack Obama

Chapter 3

Compassionate Capitalism

If you pay attention to mainstream media, you might have noticed there is a lot of talk implying that capitalism and the free enterprise system are bad things. The argument is, the rich keep getting richer while the poor keep getting poorer. According to one report, the wealthiest 1% of American households own 40% of the country's wealth.

Based on that statistic alone it's no wonder why politicians like using the wealth gap as platforms for their campaigns and then try to convince voters they can somehow close it and help voters somehow become wealthy. It's generally politicians who promote the idea that capitalism is bad to try to secure votes, but I can assure you closing the wealth gap will never be accomplished through political regulations or new laws alone. Without question, the government can play a role and we need to hold our government accountable to help eradicate social ills like poverty, but ultimately creating wealth has very little to do with politicians or politics.

So, the question we must ask ourselves as NFEs is this: Are capitalism and the Free Enterprise system a good thing or a bad thing?

Before I answer the question, let's take a stroll back in time and look at how this country became wealthy and how capitalism has positively impacted America. I must admit this is just my perception, it has not been thoroughly researched and it should not be taken objectively as true. It's simply how I see the evolution of capitalism.

In 1776, a Scottish economist named Adam Smith wrote a book titled *The Wealth of Nations*, which was published, interestingly, approximately the same time America was declaring its independence. Smith argued that the production of wealth would increase dramatically if individuals were allowed to pursue their self-interests, with little interference from government. And in serving their own interests, individuals would serve the public interest, unconsciously, as if guided by an "unseen hand." Better the unseen hand than the hand of the State said Smith.

In some ways, one might argue that Smith's book triggered the Free Enterprise system. Instead of relying on governments, individuals would now take complete responsibility for creating wealth. As a result, capitalism was triggered and pretty soon, people were taking advantage of the free enterprise system.

People like Henry Ford, who not only became the first person in this country to mass produce cars, but he also perfected the assembly line process which was eventually used in most manufacturing companies. This set-in motion a huge chain of events that laid the foundation for this country's economy to grow.

Next came the California Gold Rush, in which hundreds of

thousands of people migrated across the United States to California in search of riches. This migration created wealth and opportunities for the west coast, which eventually became one of the most affluent states in the country.

Then came the industrial revolution, which was driven in part by Andrew Carnegie. Mr. Carnegie built the Carnegie Steel Company, which he sold to J.P. Morgan in 1901 for 480 million dollars. It then became the U.S. Steel Corporation, which resulted in Pittsburgh becoming a hub for steel products and manufacturing. At one point he was considered one of the richest men in the world.

After that, J. Paul Getty positively impacted the American economy by opening the Getty Oil Company, which created an oil and gas empire, triggering the energy and fossil fuel industries. In 1966, the Guinness Book of World Records listed him as the world's richest private citizen.

The Digital Revolution was the shift from mechanical technology to digital technology, which caused an explosion in computer technology and computer companies. The primary focus was on hardware and this new industry launched the computer revolution, with companies like Dell, IBM, and Apple, who created countless millionaires.

The computer revolution then opened the door to the tech revolution, as entrepreneurs began to focus on software used with hardware. It was the tech revolution that triggered the Dot-Com boom, which turned the Internet into one of the greatest wealth creators the world has ever seen.

I believe we are currently in the Information Revolution. As I look at this list, I see the evolution of capitalism, which is culminating into the potential of unlimited wealth for anyone who is willing to put forth the effort. If we continue on the same trajectory that we've been on for the past 100 years, there will be absolutely no limits to the amount of wealth an individual can create.

So, let's get back to my original question: Is capitalism a good thing or a bad thing? My direct answer is capitalism is beyond the shadow of a doubt a very good thing. Without capitalism, America would not be one of the wealthiest countries in the world. I truly resonate with Barack Obama's quote: "I believe that the free enterprise system is the greatest engine of prosperity the world's ever known." The free enterprise system and the American dream is what I believe makes America such an amazing place to live, and despite mainstream media, I personally am extremely optimistic about the future of this country.

Of course, there will be naysayers and haters who will say things like "if capitalism is such a good thing then why is the country in such a mess?" or "why do only rich people believe in capitalism?" or how about: "if capitalism is so great why are there so many poor people?"

My answer is simple, the problem isn't capitalism, the problem is with the capitalist! As I see it, most capitalists/entrepreneurs are trapped in receiving financial compensation in exchange for their products and services. In other words, they are driven by greed and the accumulation of money and material possessions. The downside of capitalism is the primary focus is on profits and the bottom line. My goal is to change that, and that's the reason I'm asking you to embrace the idea of "compassionate capitalism."

Contrary to what most people may believe, it is absolutely possible to make money (and lots of it) while making a difference and caring about the world. To stay in business, a company has to make money and make a profit. However, from my perspective, capitalism can be combined with compassion and when you really care about your customers you will automatically improve your bottom line.

The good news is I believe more and more entrepreneurs are embracing this idea. According to Dictionary.com, a social entrepreneur is a "person who establishes an enterprise with the aim of solving social problems or effecting social change." Although most social entrepreneurs launch nonprofit organizations, the trend is shifting to profitable companies who are committed to changing the world while at the same time, making a profit.

I personally believe that the next wave of successful entrepreneurs will be *social* entrepreneurs. There is already a trend occurring, which supports my belief.

For example, have you ever heard of a guy named Muhammad Yunus? Muhammad is a Bangladeshi social entrepreneur, banker, economist, and civil society leader who was awarded the Nobel Peace Prize for founding the Grameen Bank and pioneering the concepts of microcredit and microfinance. These loans are given to entrepreneurs too poor to qualify for traditional bank loans. In 2006, Yunus and the Grameen Bank were jointly awarded the Nobel Peace Prize "for their efforts through microcredit to create economic and social development." Amazingly, 97 percent of his customers are women and even more astonishing is the minuscule default rate on his loans, which is only 2%. Muhammad is a social entrepreneur with a big heart, lots of compassion, and a very profitable bank.

As an author and publisher, I have to share the story of Better World Books. Founded in 2002 by Notre Dame grads Xavier Helgesen, Chris "Kreece" Fuchs, and Jeff Kurtzman, Better World's mission is to maximize the value of every book out there and to help promote literacy around the world. The company works by reusing or recycling books through sales on their website and donations to schools, and so far, they have used 84 million volumes to raise $12.1 million for literacy funding. The company attributes its success to using a "triple bottom line" model, caring not only about profits but also about the social and environmental impact of everything they do.

One of the most fascinating social entrepreneurs I've read about is a guy named Keller Rinaudo. His company is called Zipline and it is based out of Rwanda. Zipline is the first company to use drones - which they call "zips" - to deliver vaccines, medicine, and blood transfusions for use in rural Rwanda. A zip zooms along at 100km/hour, dropping off its cargo with a small parachute. Zipline is partnering with the Rwanda government in 20 hospitals and health centers, providing urgent medical supplies for millions of people.

These are just a couple of examples of social entrepreneurs. If you would like to read more, be sure to check out the book *The Business of Good* by serial and social entrepreneur Jason Haber. In the book he intertwines case studies and anecdotes that show how social entrepreneurship is creating jobs, growing the economy, and ultimately changing the world.

Another interesting trend is philanthropy, which in a way is a form of social entrepreneurship. As the list of millionaires and billionaires continues to grow, there is a movement among the financially elite to commit to using their money for making the world a better place. One example of this is The Giving Pledge which is a philanthropic initiative started by Warren Buffett and Bill & Melinda Gates. The Giving Pledge is a commitment by the world's wealthiest individuals and families to dedicate the majority of their wealth to giving back. Of course, wealthy individuals have been donating money for hundreds of years and philanthropy isn't something new. What makes the Giving Pledge so unique is the members of this group are committed to making sure their wealth is distributed to charity after their deaths, instead of being passed down to their children or family members.

There is also evidence of this trend with pro athletes and celebrities. In June of 2018, basketball superstar Lebron James opened an eight-million-dollar public school in Akron, Ohio. The students receive free meals, free bikes, and free college tuition. The first group of 240 kids were 3rd and 4th graders, and the goal is to add an additional grade level each year until they reach 8th grade. Since the school considers education to be not just for the pupil, but for the whole family, it offers GED classes and job placement assistance for parents and guardians.

There are countless celebrities involved in using their wealth to make a difference in the world. Actor Leonardo DiCaprio is a workhorse for environmental causes, raising at least $61 million for more than 65 climate-change, biodiversity, and conservation programs since 1998. Public records show he has donated about $3.2 million of his own money.

From my perspective, as more and more people wake up to who they really are and embrace compassionate capitalism, the engine of capitalism will shift from focusing on making a profit to focusing on making a difference, and thereby assist in the eradication of the vast majority of social ills around the globe.

The point of sharing these stories is to challenge you to think about capitalism and how it can be used for the greater good. The purpose of this book is to provide you with insights on becoming the best entrepreneur you can possibly be and being clear on your values around money is extremely important for you to understand.

And so now I would like you to become self-introspective and ask yourself a few questions.

#1. Which is more important, your bottom-line or making sure your customers receive value and quality from your products or services?

#2. If you were a billionaire, what causes would you support and how would you support them?

#3. If you ran a billion-dollar company, would paying yourself 150 million dollars a year be okay?

There are no right or wrong answers. Simply be honest with yourself and think about your answers.

As mentioned at the beginning of this chapter, I believe it's important for all entrepreneurs to seek spiritual compensation first with their businesses. To do so, you must embrace spiritual principles and understand Universal laws to truly become an NFE.

Truth be told, on the surface, capitalism really isn't spiritual - it's a man-made construct used as a guide to create and distribute wealth. But as more and more entrepreneurs embrace compassionate capitalism, I believe it can evolve into a spiritual practice that embraces Universal laws, which can lead entrepreneurs to create joy, passion, and profits in their business.

So now let's talk about a few of the Universal laws about money.

Albert Einstein once stated: "Everything is energy, that's just the way that it is. Match the frequency with the reality that you want to create and there is no way you cannot create that reality. It can be no other way. This isn't philosophy, this is physics."

Nikola Tesla said: "If you want to understand the Universe,

think in terms of energy, frequency and vibration."

The first law you should embrace is **Everything Is Energy**. Science has shown if you break down matter to its smallest component you'll find the smallest particle of matter really isn't a particle, it's simply a wave of energy vibrating at a high rate of speed. When you slow down the vibration of this energy you create solid matter.

If you accept my premise that you are a spiritual being having a human experience, the acceptance of this law is the key to your success. Simply stated, you are an energetic spiritual being. As such, you have the ability to create anything or any reality you choose. When you grasp the concept that "Everything is Energy" it should empower you to understand *you* are the source of every experience of your life. Everything that shows up in your life is a reflection of the Energy you're expressing.

Which leads us to the next law, the **Law of Attraction**. Following the law that everything is energy, the law of attraction is exactly how it sounds. Based on your energy vibration you attract everything and every experience - good, bad, or indifferent - into your life. If you aren't happy with what is showing up in your life you must be willing to change your internal energy before you see anything change in your external reality.

When you fully grasp this principle, it allows you to become 100% responsible for everything that shows up in your life. Although it may be difficult, accepting this truth will give you your power back and keep you from ever feeling like a victim. Although it may appear other people, the government, your ex-wife/husband, or even God is responsible for your misfortune and unhappiness, the truth is, you are always 100% responsible for everything that shows up, so you might as well accept this truth and be willing to act to change anything you do not like. And the only way to do that is to go within and change your inner energy vibration (more on this in the next chapter).

The next law I want to share is **The Universe is Infinite**. We live in a society and culture that promotes the idea that there is a lack or scarcity of everything. This fear of scarcity drives companies to constantly compete with others to win customers out of fear that there isn't enough of them. Countries have wars over oil out of fear that we will one day run out of oil. Governments reject immigration out of fear that immigrants will create a shortage of jobs for their residents. Fear and scarcity drive the consciousness of the world, but I would like to suggest that this fear is unwarranted. The reason I say this is because I believe the Universe is Infinite and there is no scarcity.

When we embrace this law, we come to understand there really is enough of everything for everyone on the planet. There is enough food to feed everyone. There are enough customers for all businesses to thrive. There are enough mineral resources to fuel us. There is enough shelter for everyone to have decent housing. There is enough water so that no one should ever be thirsty.

There is no such thing as scarcity because the Universe is Infinite. The reason these scarcities exist is because, collectively, we believe in insufficiency and scarcity. When we shift our focus away from scarcity and place our attention on abundance we lay the groundwork to build companies that thrive.

Once again, I hear the naysayers screaming loudly; "oh boy, he's one of those head-in-the-clouds, pie-in-the-sky, airy-fairy, idealistic liberals." To which I reply: "whatever the mind can conceive, you can achieve if you truly believe." I believe in abundance and from this belief comes my optimism and idealism. As irrational as it may seem, grasping the idea that the Universe is Infinite and then acting in conjunction with this belief creates the experience of abundance in my reality.

The final Universal Law is **Thoughts Become Things** and I mean this literally. If you go back to the first law, which is Everything Is Energy, it shouldn't be a stretch to embrace this law. If everything is energy, then that means thoughts are energy too. Therefore, what you think about you bring about. Put another way, *thoughts held in mind creates likes of its kind.* This is the reason positive thinking is so important. What if you knew with absolute certainty that every thought you had was creative? Would you pay more attention to what you are thinking? The good book says; "As a man thinketh in his heart, so shall he be." Which speaks directly to this particular law.

Of course, it takes a lot more than just thinking to build a business, create a great relationship, or have inner peace, but it all begins with thought. Everything that has ever been created begins as a simple thought in someone's mind, so it's important for you to embrace this law as you're building a business or building a life.

So, these are the four primary laws you must embrace as an NFE:

1. Everything Is Energy
2. The Law of Attraction
3. The Universe is Infinite
4. Thoughts Become Things

The challenge and opportunity is to understand and embrace these Universal Laws. You must accept the fact that the Universe is perfect by design and you are an expression of that perfection. Therefore, you have an infinite capacity to create anything you want. It can be a home-based business or a billion-dollar enterprise, but it all begins with your willingness to accept these laws, dream big, and do not let anyone or anything keep you from accomplishing your dream.

I'm reminded of the story of J.K. Rowling, the author of the Harry Potter books, and also has a net worth of a billion dollars in 2004. Ms. Rowling was a single mother on welfare when she began writing the first Harry Potter book. She battled depression and poverty before she finally secured a publishing deal. Eventually, she became the first billion-dollar author and her books have sold over 500 million copies around the globe.

She is recognized as one of the most generous and compassionate philanthropists in the world and she relinquished her billionaire status because she has given much of her money to charity.

She practices compassionate capitalism, and she is a role model and inspiration to millions around the world.

I'm not sure if she would agree with the four primary Universal Laws that I mentioned, but without question, she has used these laws to reach the pinnacle of success. Her faith in herself and her writing and her willingness to trust her own heart and pursue her dream should serve as an inspiration to all entrepreneurs who are chasing a dream. She epitomizes compassionate capitalism by sharing her gifts, receiving financial compensation for her products and services, and being willing to support others through her generous financial gifts.

To me, she is a hero and definitely someone I strive to emulate.

So, rest assured there is absolutely nothing wrong with making lots and lots of money. Capitalism can be a good thing, and you should not feel guilty in wanting to make a lot of money. Just keep your priorities in order and know that the more money you make the more you can help others. If you choose to become a compassionate capitalist then I suggest you use her life as a template for your own and commit to sharing your gifts, creating products and services that make a difference, and ensuring your company commits to making a difference while making a profit. When you do these things, I assure you that you will be authentically successful and joyful.

"When you learn to quiet the noise of your mind and move into the silence of your heart, then you will hear the voice of your Soul."

Michael Taylor

Chapter 4
Trust Your Inner Wisdom

Have you ever been deeply moved by something beautiful? Maybe it was a sunset or holding a newborn baby. Maybe it was a loving gaze by someone you cared deeply about. Or maybe you were out in nature and experienced a deep sense of reverence and awe for the majesty of Mother Nature. Have you ever experienced the feeling of joy at such a deep level that it literally brought you to tears?

Have you ever pondered how a leatherback sea turtle that travels more than 12,000 miles between Indonesia and the United States knows how to return to the place of its birth to lay eggs and give birth to the next generation of turtles?

Or what about the great wildebeest migration in southeastern Africa, where more than 2 million wildebeest and 200,000 zebras and gazelle make an annual circular trip of more than 1,800 miles.

How do they know how to do that?

Or what about human sperm? How does it know to locate the egg and embed itself into it so that life can begin? And even more amazing, how does that simple act of impregnating the egg grow into this amazing thing called a human being?

How?

For me, the answer is simple. There are a Divine Energy and Intelligence that permeate the Universe. This intelligence is the source of all creation and it is inherent in everything in the Universe. It is this Intelligence that drives animal migration and guides the sperm to find the egg. It is this intelligence that is responsible for all of life and it is the source of our feelings of love, beauty, joy, and awe. As the great Master Teacher Yoda put it: "For my ally is The Force, and a powerful ally it is. Life creates it, makes it grow. Its energy surrounds us and binds us. Luminous beings are we, not this crude matter. You must feel the Force around you; here, between you, me, the tree, the rock, everywhere, yes!"

When we look at the animal kingdom we describe this intelligence as instinct. From a human being's perspective, it can be defined as intuition.

One of my favorite books on this subject is One Mind by Dr. Larry Dossey. In the book, he theorizes an inspiring view of consciousness that may reshape our destiny. Dossey's premise is that all individual minds are part of an infinite, collective dimension of consciousness he calls the One Mind. This state - which we can all access - explains phenomena as diverse as epiphanies, creative breakthroughs, premonitions of danger or disaster, near-death experiences, communication with other species and with the dead, reincarnation, the movement of herds, flocks, and schools, and remote healing.

Dossey presents his theory in easily digestible, bite-sized vignettes. Through engaging stories, fascinating research, and brilliant insights from great thinkers throughout history, readers will explore the outer reaches of human consciousness, discover a new way to interpret the great mysteries of our experience, and learn how to develop the empathy necessary to engender more love, peace, and collective awareness. The result is a rich new understanding of what it means to be human and a renewed hope that we can successfully confront the challenges we face at this crossroads in human history. Even before publication, One Mind drew praise from the finest minds of our time. It has been heralded as a "landmark", a "brilliant synthesis", a "magnum opus", a "feast" of ideas, "compelling", "gripping", and a "major shift in our understanding of consciousness" (description from Amazon.com).

This book has definitely influenced my life and my thinking about intuition and how to use it. I've always been a huge fan of Dr. Dossey's work and this book is my favorite. One of the most fascinating stories he shares in the book is about a family who lost their dog approximately 2500 miles away from their home. Miraculously, the dog was able to find its way home. There are lots of stories of animals being able to find their way home over long distances, but when put into the context of Dr. Dossey's One Mind theory, the story really struck home for me and confirmed what I've always believed: this Infinite Intelligence that permeates the Universe intimately connects us all.

Since listening to your intuition is so important, I wanted to take this opportunity to share some things I have learned about intuition and hopefully provide you with some insights that will help you to get in touch with your own intuition, and then use it to guide you to build your business and to your ultimate destiny.

So, let's begin by defining what intuition really is. Webster's dictionary describes it as:

> *a natural ability or power that makes it possible to know something without any proof or evidence: a feeling that guides a person to act a certain way without fully understanding why.*

In American culture, intuition has usually been associated with women. Have you ever heard the term "woman's intuition"? The truth is, intuition has absolutely nothing to do with gender. I believe men are just as intuitive as women, but unfortunately, in our culture, men have been conditioned to believe that they aren't.

Although it's somewhat difficult to fully define intuition with words, take a moment and ask yourself if you've experienced any of these situations:

- You were thinking about someone when the phone rings and it turns out to be the person you were thinking about.
- You had a funny feeling in your gut that told you not to do something, even though you wanted to, and then you listened to your gut and it turned out to be right.
- Something happened to you at just the right moment in a way that you didn't expect, but it helped

you reach one of your goals.

- You were thinking about a friend or someone you care about that you haven't seen in a while, and then you ran into them in a store or some unexpected place.
- You were struggling with a problem and all of a sudden, a solution popped into your head without you even thinking about it.

If you've experienced any of these situations, you've actually used your intuition. Referring to the quote, "*a feeling that guides a person to act a certain way without fully understanding why*" that feeling or knowing that you had without knowing why was your intuition.

If you accept what I said in the previous chapters about The Infinite Energy and Intelligence, then another way to look at intuition is simply as the universe's way of communicating directly with you. I believe we all have direct access to this intelligence, but unfortunately, very few people will tap into it. Since you're reading this book, I'm going to assume you would like to access your intuition, so let me share an article I truly resonate with. It's called *5 Ways to Help You Get in Touch with Your Intuition* by Christina Lattimer of People Discovery Magazine, and I personally have used these five steps in my own life.

1. Meditation is giving you a holiday from the clamor of your daily thoughts and stream of information. It is finding the gap between your thoughts and staying there. Silent and observant, you can watch your thoughts without attaching yourself to them. It is allowing your intuition or your unconscious wisdom space. Through meditation, your intuition may come to you in different ways, either through thoughts, ideas, or an encounter with someone or something. Use meditation to be open to whatever comes up.

2. Contemplation is also about clearing your mind, but for me, it is more purposeful. You may have a problem or a situation where you're not sure what to do, or don't know what the solution is. Ask clearly what the problem is, and then simply observe the problem from different angles and instead of actively thinking about the information, let thoughts come up. Often, you can be inspired by a solution, although sometimes the emerging solution isn't immediate. It can pop up at any time.

3. Writing is extremely powerful if you are disturbed or upset, even if you aren't sure why. Write down how you are feeling, why you are feeling that way, and then ask your intuition how you can look at the situation differently. Then write down different ideas, until you find a perspective which feels good and you can believe. Writing is about telling the story of what is going on in your mind and giving you an opportunity to *see it from a better perspective.* The true trick is to ask your intuition how to perceive the situation so that you can be at peace with it. It's not about repressing feelings though. Feelings are a great emotional guidance system, and it's important to let them come up and help to inform the writing process.

4. Listen to Music – You are better aligned with your intuition or higher self when you are feeling good. You know you are feeling good when you are in touch with appreciation, gratitude, love, and laughter. Listening to music you love can quickly help you get into those places which feel so good. A daily dose of music you love can definitely align you with your intuition.

5. Going outside – Whether it's fresh winter air or warm summer sunshine, getting away from the clutter of a busy workplace or a demanding home can clear your mind and give you space which you might not otherwise give yourself. Staying in the present moment and clearing your mind while you are outside is a must. It's no good getting out into the open and taking all your clamorous thoughts with you.

I ran across a very informative article titled *10 Things Highly Intuitive People Do Differently*, by Carolyn Gregoire of the Huffington Post Magazine, which shared some amazing insights about intuition. I would like to share her 10 things, and then share my comments about them:

1. They listen to that inner voice
2. They take time for solitude
3. They create
4. They practice mindfulness
5. They observe everything
6. They listen to their bodies
7. They connect deeply with others
8. They pay attention to their dreams
9. They enjoy plenty of downtime
10. They mindfully let go of negative emotions

1. They listen to that inner voice

This is the key to developing your intuition. The more you

listen to it, the more you will be able to recognize it. I now trust my intuition more than I trust my logical mind. If something doesn't feel right, yet makes logical sense, I will pay more attention to the feeling than I will the logical thought. My inner voice is the guiding force in all my decisions.

2. They take time for solitude

I am naturally a loner. This does not mean that I'm anti-social, it simply means that I always make time for personal solitude. As a matter of fact, I am an extroverted guy who really loves being around people, but I also value my solitude and love spending time alone. As a happily married man, I love spending time with my wife, but she also recognizes my need for solitary time and she allows me to have it on a regular basis without feeling neglected. It's an extremely important part of my life.

3. They create

I am highly creative and absolutely love creating new things. Whether it's writing books, developing programs, or creating motivational speeches, I have to express my creativity. As I tap into my intuition it gives me access to an infinite amount of creative ideas.

4. They practice mindfulness

Mindfulness is the practice of being aware. It's about paying attention and being in the present moment. It means being in touch with your thoughts, feelings, and physical sensations, and recognizing that what happens to me doesn't matter as much as what I do with what happens to me.

5. They observe everything

I try to maintain a childlike curiousness in everything I do. This keeps me open-minded and aware of everything around me. I'm like a sponge in any environment, simply taking in everything that's going around me and being able to make conscious choices in how I react to those things.

6. They listen to their bodies

Being in touch with my physical body is a high priority for me. I enjoy working out and taking care of my body and I have learned to listen to it when it sends me signals that something may be wrong. I also get a yearly physical, which gives me an idea of what's going on in my body to make sure that I prevent any problems that may arise. I'm a firm believer in the philosophy that an ounce of prevention is worth a pound of cure.

7. They connect deeply with others

Having deep and intimate connected relationships is the foundation of my happiness. Learning how to do this took years of deep inner emotional and psychological work, but the results have been amazing. Learning to open my heart to others to give and receive love brings me great joy.

8. They pay attention to their dreams

Having dreams and goals are another driving force in my life. As an entrepreneur, I am constantly seeking new ways to grow my business and build my legacy. All my entrepreneurial pursuits are driven by my commitment to making the world a better place by sharing my unique gifts and talents with the world.

9. They enjoy plenty of downtime

Downtime for me is watching movies, listening to '70s soul music, and reading my favorite comic strip, Calvin & Hobbes. It's also spending time in silence through my meditation practice. I make a point to do at least one of these every single day.

10. They mindfully let go of negative emotions

I am a huge advocate of personal development programs that help heal emotional and psychological trauma. I have spent a considerable amount of time, energy, and effort letting go of negative emotions and as a result, it has brought me deep inner peace and serenity, and it has definitely connected me to my intuition.

If you make the commitment to yourself to get in touch with your intuition, you too can enjoy all ten of these things. Anyone can do this; they simply have to make a commitment to access their intuition and make it a high priority in their lives.

There are countless benefits to connecting with your intuition, but by far I believe the greatest benefit is becoming aware of divine synchronicities. When and if you truly tap into your intuition it will serve as a guidance system for your life. When you do this, you will begin to recognize how unexplainable coincidences are actually divine synchronicities set in motion by The Source, and your intuition helps you to recognize them.

Rather than try to define synchronicities, I would like to share a series of synchronicities that confirm for me The

Source was constantly working in my favor to support me in manifesting a lifelong dream of mine.

More than twenty years ago I had a dream to run a company that would develop self-esteem building programs for children. I had no experience in developing programs and I had no idea how to start a non-profit organization that would implement these programs. Despite my lack of knowledge and experience, I decided I would start a company anyway. After several years of failure, I held on to my dream of building this company, but the reality was my life had actually fallen apart. I got to a point where I was homeless for a couple of years, and despite the challenges, I still held on to the dream.

Approximately seven years after I had conceived the idea for my company, I had no luck in getting it funded. Despite this, I held on to my dream and continued to look for ways to bring my dream to reality. During this time, I was renting a rundown one-room apartment and I was making minimum wage working at a video store. I had a bicycle for transportation and I could barely make ends meet. But somehow, I intuitively knew that I would eventually figure out a way to raise the money for my company.

One day while working at the video store, a man came in with his children and asked me if I could make a recommendation for some movies for them to watch. I made the recommendation and he took them home to view them with his children.

A couple of days later he came back and told me that his children absolutely loved the movies and he wanted to thank me for the recommendations. He then became a regular customer and would always come in on the weekends and pick up movies to watch.

One evening he came in and we started talking, and somehow, we began talking about challenges in life. He then told me he was dealing with a major challenge because he had recently been diagnosed with cancer. During our conversation, I mentioned some of the challenges I had gone through, and I suggested to him that no matter how difficult challenges might be, there is always a positive lesson for us to learn within them.

When I said that, he smiled at me and said he completely agreed. He told me how his diagnosis had challenged him to really take a deep look at his life, and since he had been diagnosed he had actually been happier with his life because for the first time he realized just how important his children were and how precious his life was. As a result of his cancer, he had become a better father and ultimately a better man.

After our conversation, we became close friends and each time he would visit we would spend some time just chatting and supporting each other.

One day I was at work with a co-worker and my friend came in and asked me for some movie recommendations. After he picked up his movies and left my co-worker asked me if I knew who he was. I told him yes and said that he was a friend of mine. My co-worker then asked me again, "Do you realize who that is?" I said yes, his name is Mike and he is a good customer and a good friend of mine.

My co-worker then informed me that he was a very wealthy businessman who owned an oil company.

The next time my friend came into the store I decided to ask him if he might be able to help me with my dream. I told him about my dream of creating the programs for kids and I asked him if there was any way that he could help out.

He then reached into his pocket and handed me one of his business cards. "Michael, whatever you're working on I would be glad to help you. Contact my secretary and make an appointment and let me see what I can do."

During this time, I was deeply involved with spiritual teachings and I had learned to keep my heart and my mind open to miracles. I didn't know how he would help me, but I intuitively knew that somehow, he would.

A few days later I met him at his office and I was pleasantly surprised to learn just how wealthy he was. His office was like something you would see on a television set. It was filled with sports memorabilia, wild animals, and pictures of my friend with former presidents and lots of famous celebrities.

I sat down and began explaining my idea to him. After I finished, he picked up the phone and contacted another wealthy businessman who was in charge of a non-profit foundation who had access to a lot of money. He told the person on the phone that I would be coming by to visit him, and that he wanted to make sure he would support my programs.

When he hung up the phone he gave me another business card and told me to make an appointment to see the guy he had just spoken with, and he assured me that the man would be able to help me in some way. I thanked him repeatedly and let him know just how much I appreciated his support. He then looked at me and said *"I want to thank you for being my friend and for listening to me and sharing your dreams with me. I believe you are going to be very successful and I'm glad that I was able to help."*

A few weeks later I met with the other businessman who loved my business idea, and a few months later I received a check for fifty thousand dollars to get my company started.

Let that sink in for a moment. I was completely broke, I had no formal education or training, I had a bicycle for transportation, and I was living in a rundown dilapidated apartment I could barely afford. Despite all these challenges I was able to receive a check for fifty thousand dollars!

A lot of people would say this was just a coincidence, or I was just lucky. I, on the other hand, recognize that this had absolutely nothing to do with luck. It was divine synchronicity that orchestrated all of the events that led to me receiving the funding. It began with my belief that I would receive the funding. Faith is defined as evidence of things unseen, and I had unwavering faith that somehow, I would be able to secure funding. It was then followed by my willingness to work extremely hard to keep my head above water while I was trying to start my company.

My faith and belief in Infinite Intelligence and myself gave me the patience and persistence to not give up, even after several years of failure. The key was my willingness to listen to my intuition and to trust that Infinite Intelligence would provide me with the guidance I needed to be at the right place at the right time to meet the right people. By relying on Infinite Intelligence 100% and being willing to combine action with faith, I was able to locate the funding to get my company started.

This is why it is so important to learn to listen to, and trust, your inner wisdom and intuition. As I've mentioned, Infinite Intelligence is constantly communicating with us through our intuition, and when we tune in and learn to connect the dots of synchronicity, it can guide us to our ultimate destiny.

So, learn to listen to your heart and connect to your intuition, and you will receive all the guidance you need to live the life of your dreams.

I'm living proof of this.

"We need to give each other the space to grow, to be ourselves, to exercise our diversity. We need to give each other space so that we may both give and receive such beautiful things as ideas, openness, dignity, joy, healing, and inclusion."

Max de Pree

Chapter 5

The Glue That Holds
Your Company Together

Have you ever worked for someone who was a real jerk? Someone who may have been controlling, argumentative, arrogant, conniving or dishonest? What was it like working for that person? Did you enjoy going to work? Were you comfortable approaching that person and asking for guidance and support? Were you loyal to that person and committed to doing your best?

Chances are the answers are a resounding 'no'. Whenever a boss is hard to work with it makes it difficult for everyone at the company to work together and ensure the company's success. The really hard part when you work for a terrible boss is that no matter how good you are and no matter how well-intentioned you may be, a truly bad boss can create a living hell for you, and there really isn't anything you can do about it unless you choose to find another job.

I once worked for a boss who was extremely insecure and intimidated by me. She was a lot younger and less experienced than I was and she found it extremely difficult to deal with these facts. Whenever I made suggestions she knew were better than what she was currently doing, she would reject them and create excuses for not implementing them. She used every opportunity to belittle me and try to make me look bad in front of other employees.

Rather than become defensive and create friction with her, I took the high road and did my very best to not let her negative attitude affect my performance. I focused on doing the very best job I could, and I even went the extra mile and did things that weren't my responsibility. One of my strongest attributes has always been customer service. Every job that I've ever had I've been recognized for providing outstanding customer service. I absolutely love helping customers!

As a result of my excellent customer service, upper management had acknowledged me because several of my customers had called in and shared how much they appreciated my service. Having customers call the main office to complement an employee is definitely a rarity in a retail environment, but I'm proud to say that it occurred on a regular basis when I worked for this company.

Of course, whenever I received compliments from the main office my manager would get jealous and vindictive and try to find ways to negate my acknowledgements. But this is how Karma works.

Remember when I said you always get back what you put out?

Despite my manager's attitude, I did not let her negativity

impact me. I maintained a positive mental attitude, didn't get defensive, and continued to provide my customers with excellent customer service. I also maintained an excellent rapport with my co-workers and was well=liked and respected by all of them.

One day my manager and I got into a heated discussion and she became so upset she called one of the district managers. When the district manager got there, he interviewed all my co-workers first and then he called me in. I gave him my side of the story and then he called in my manager.

After speaking with her, he left and said he would be back the following day to let us know what would be done to try to resolve our dispute.

Interestingly enough, they ended up demoting my manager and moving her to another store, and they promoted me to an assistant manager and brought a new manager in.

Once again, I have to reference Karma. I did not allow my bad manager's attitude to impact my behavior or my thoughts and actions. I knew that as long as I focused my attention on the energy I was giving off, the Universe would support me, and I would be okay. On the other hand, my former manager reaped what she had sown. Her negative, judgmental and angry energy resulted in her demotion.

As an entrepreneur, you must understand the importance of relationships. Relationships are the glue that binds your company together and if you do not nurture strong bonds, your business cannot survive. As the leader, you must understand that your team will always follow your lead.

A corporate culture is the result and expression of the entrepreneur's deepest held values and beliefs. If you want to create a culture of connection, openness, diversity, transformation, fun, and profitability, it is imperative that you as the entrepreneur exude and express those qualities and values. This is how corporate Karma works. The energy that you as the leader give off permeates the entire organization.

A powerful way to understand the importance of relationships in business is through the metaphor of team sports. There are 4 components of every team sport:

1. Game
2. Coach
3. Players
4. Culture

1. The Game. First of all, you must fully understand the game you are playing. You must know how to play, and you must be willing to follow the rules. The rules aren't there to restrict you, they're there to ensure you know exactly how to play, and if you do not play by those rules you will be penalized.

2. The Coach. The coach's job is to completely understand the rules of the game, so he can make sure the team plays by them. It's also his job to make sure every player plays the game to the best of their ability. Their job is to bring out the best in each player, so they work together to create the best team possible.

3. The Players. The player's job is to express their unique gifts and talents with the team. Each player brings a certain skill set and talent to the team, and when the players are given the opportunity to contribute their talents and combine them with other team members, the team becomes one cohesive unit with a single goal of making the team the best it can be.

4. The Culture. The culture is really the essence of the team. It is the values, qualities, and beliefs that the collective team adheres to. It is the "energy" of the collective team that translates in to how the players play and the coach coaches.

In 2017, the Houston Astros won the World Series Baseball Championship. It was the first time in the city's history to do so and it was a very proud moment for the city to experience. Their championship was the result of hiring the right coach who had an amazing group of players who accepted a culture of excellence and played well together.

So, what does baseball have to do with running a business?

Everything!

Running a successful business requires the same four components as building a championship team. The game you're playing is business, as an entrepreneur you are the coach, your employees are the players, and your corporate culture is the essence of your business.

To build a championship business it all begins with you. You must first understand your business and your industry. Next, you must recognize that you are the coach and the soul of your business. Next, you must be willing to "coach" your employees, so they can express their unique gifts and talents, and finally you must cultivate a culture of excellence, so your company can thrive.

So, the next question you should be asking yourself is "how can I become the best possible coach for my business?"

Herein lies the greatest challenge for all entrepreneurs - figuring out how to become the best entrepreneur that they can be. This is the primary reason I've written this book, as a powerful resource for becoming the best "coach" of your business.

So, are you truly committed to becoming the best entrepreneur you're capable of becoming? Are you willing to learn how to be the best coach for your team?

If you answered yes, the key to being the best entrepreneur possible begins with knowing who you truly are! At the beginning of this book, I mentioned you are a spiritual being having a human experience. I also mentioned you are a three-part being consisting of mind, body, and spirit. It is absolutely imperative you become aware of these fundamental ideas.

You must accept you are a human being first, whose purpose has chosen to manifest as an entrepreneur. Being an entrepreneur is something you do to live your purpose, it isn't who and what you are. It's really just a label you choose to wear, but rest assured you are not a label.

So, let's shift our attention away from being an entrepreneur for now and focus on how you can become the best human being you can possibly become. So how do you do that?

First of all, you must understand and embrace the Mirror Principle. The mirror principle means:

> *"The quality of your relationship with yourself influences the quality of your relationships with everyone and everything else. Your relationship with you is reflected in every other relationship there is."*

This is a Universal truth that you must accept. Every relationship begins and ends with you, and the relationship you have with yourself is going to dictate how all of the other relationships you are engaged in will turn out.

In the hit song "Man in The Mirror" by Michael Jackson, there is a line which says: "I'm starting with the man in the mirror and I'm asking him to change his ways. And no message could have been any clearer if you want to make the world a better place take a look at yourself and make a change."

These are words to live by and the foundation of being truly happy with yourself and with your life. You must be willing to start with the man/woman in the mirror and ask him/her if they're ready to change.

If you are, a great place to begin is by making peace with your past. This is by far the most challenging part about being human. It takes courage, discipline, vulnerability, compassion, patience, and persistence, but for those who are willing to do this, they will be rewarded with purpose, passion, joy, and fulfillment.

I'd like to share a quote from author and spiritual teacher Iyanla Vanzant that fully embodies why making peace with your past is so important. This powerful quote holds the key to your happiness and I suggest you read it slowly (and several times) and intently so you fully grasp the implications of its message.

> *"Until you heal the wounds of your past, you are going to bleed. You can bandage the bleeding with food, with alcohol, with drugs, with work, with cigarettes, with sex; but eventually, it will all ooze through and stain your life. You must find the strength to open the wounds, stick your hands inside, pull out the core of the pain that is holding you in your past, the memories, and make peace with them."*

Herein lies the key to becoming the best human being you can possibly be. What I've learned over the last twenty years is we must be willing to heal our hearts and make peace with our past if we truly want to be happy. We can read all the self-help books in the world and listen to audio programs or go to seminars with motivational speakers, but if we fail to carry out our healing work we will subconsciously sabotage our lives and ultimately keep ourselves from being completely happy.

Amazingly, there are some people who don't believe their childhood can actually have an adverse effect on their adult lives. Have you ever heard someone say their parents used to beat them when they were little, yet they still turned out okay? This statement is a defense mechanism keeping people trapped in their pain, and they will rationalize their traumatic childhoods had no effect on them whatsoever. The truth is, if you remember being beaten as a child and you have not done any healing work, I can assure you that it will have an effect on your life today.

If you remember what I said in the preceding chapters about the subconscious mind, this should make sense to you. There are negative beliefs you may have stored about yourself that could be causing you to unconsciously sabotage your life. This can show up as failed relationships, anxiety, depression, anger issues, or an overall feeling that something is simply missing from your life.

The key to making peace with your past lies in your willingness to heal any emotional scars you may be carrying from your childhood. Healing your heart is the key to making peace with your past. Psychologists will tell you that at their core, all addictions have an unresolved emotional conflict, which simply means there are emotional wounds that need to be healed.

What Iyanla Vanzant meant when she said *"You must find the strength to open the wounds, stick your hands inside, pull out the core of the pain that is holding you in your past, the memories, and make peace with them"* is that it is your responsibility to look within your own heart and find where the pain is, and be willing to heal that pain.

There is a powerful scene in the movie Star Wars, in which Luke Skywalker is being trained by the Master Teacher Yoda. In the scene, Yoda tells Luke that he must enter into a dark cave to face his demons and ultimately become a Jedi Knight. As Luke begins to look into the cave, he turns to Yoda and asks: "What's in the cave?" To which Yoda replies; "Only what you take with you." As Luke goes into the cave he is confronted by his nemesis, Darth Vader. Darth Vader is the antagonist in the movie who embraces "The Dark Side." As Darth Vader approaches, Luke pulls out his Light Saber and fights him. After a brief battle, Luke chops off Darth Vader's head and it appears that he has defeated the bad guy. As Luke looks at the severed head, smoke suddenly issues from the helmet Vader is wearing. As the smoke clears, Luke looks inside the helmet and sees his own face.

The symbolism of this scene speaks directly to the importance of making peace with your past. Luke Skywalker represents the good in every human being, and his training with the Master represents the importance of having teachers to guide us on our personal growth journeys to find the good that is within us. The dark cave represents your subconscious mind that stores all your erroneous negative beliefs about yourself. It is the place where fear resides, and we must be willing to enter the cave if we truly want to make peace with our past and not live in fear.

Darth Vader represents the parts of ourselves we are sometimes afraid to look at. He symbolizes our shadows, which are the parts of ourselves we sometimes hide, suppress, or deny. The battle represents the struggle we must go through in order to shed light on the dark places in our minds and hearts that keep us from expressing who we really are. Cutting off Darth Vader's head and then Luke seeing his own face represents facing our demons within and then allowing the dark parts of ourselves to die so we can be resurrected into who we truly are.

The key is to remember what Yoda said about what's in the cave: "only what you take with you." This means the darkness we perceive is only in our minds. The so-called darkness is simply erroneous beliefs we hold about ourselves, and when we become courageous enough to face our own inner darkness, that part of us dies and the real part of us awakens.

There are some people who prescribe to the idea that you do not have to address your childhood wounds in order to be successful and happy. They believe it does not do any good to "dig up" old hurts. I completely disagree with this way of thinking. I believe it is absolutely imperative you are willing to look at the dark events in your life and are willing to shed light on them. If you are unwilling to do so, those dark places will eventually sabotage your happiness.

There is a term called "spiritual bypassing", which means a person refuses to heal their inner wounds because they have accepted a specific religious teaching that says God can heal you. I used to hold that belief. At one time I thought if I prayed enough and followed religious dogma and doctrine, then I would eventually become happy. My own experience has taught me otherwise. It wasn't until I became courageous enough to make peace with my past and deal with some childhood trauma that I was able to heal my heart and become genuinely happy.

When I decided I wanted to heal my wounds I was introduced to a man named John Bradshaw who facilitated a program called "Healing Your Inner Child." In one of his workshops, I learned how my abusive childhood was at the core of all the dysfunction in my life. I learned I had abandonment issues as a result of being separated from my mom when I was six years old, and I also learned that for the majority of my adult life I was driven by a deep sense of shame. It was my internal feelings of shame that drove me to be successful. I worked really hard to gain other people's approval because deep down I didn't feel worthy.

Although it was extremely difficult, I made the choice to heal my heart and make peace with my past. I took Iyanla's advice and found the strength to open my wounds and stick my hands inside and pull out the core of my pain keeping me trapped in my past - and I made peace with them.

As a result of doing this work, I can honestly admit in this very moment I am happier today than I've ever been in my life. It definitely wasn't easy, but I can assure you it was worth it.

I hope you will take some time and really think about what

I've just shared. Do not make the same mistakes I did in believing that thinking positive all the time will solve all your problems. Of course, there is absolutely nothing wrong with being positive, and I am still a huge advocate of positive thinking. The key is to make sure you aren't hiding behind positivity because of some unresolved emotional pain the way I did.

If you are committed to making peace with your past and are looking for some ways to do so, let me make a few suggestions for you to consider. First of all, I think it's really important you are willing to seek support if needed. I realize there is a lot of negative stigma attached in seeking support, but this is a sign of strength, not weakness when you choose to seek help.

Here are a few things for you to consider if you are truly ready to make peace with your past.

1. Therapy

There is nothing wrong with seeking out a good therapist to support you in dealing with any emotional challenges you may be facing. Our society has conditioned us to believe we are supposed to carry the weight of the world on our shoulders and not seek support, but this simply isn't true. We all need support at one time or another, so if you've been looking for ways to help you make peace with your past, a good therapist may be exactly what you need.

I would like to share an article I wrote a while ago that shares my first experience with therapy. My hope is it will give you some insight on how difficult and challenging it might be, but also to inspire you to take the first step if you think you will benefit from therapy. The article is titled "Men's Emotional Healing."

In 1989 I had a series of traumatic experiences that were beginning to take their toll. My divorce and separation from my kids were extremely painful and had begun to negatively impact my life. I had slipped into a deep state of depression and was barely able to function on a daily basis. As my depression deepened, I went into isolation, where I literally shut myself off from the outside world.

Although I was able to go to work and function in that capacity, I was completely disconnected from any social settings. I was not dating, and I did not socialize with my friends. I also had difficulty sleeping. I would rarely eat, and I had begun to lose weight, which was rare for me, as a former personal trainer who took excellent care of my physical body. After several months I began to have fleeting thoughts of suicide, and it appeared that my situation was hopeless. In an effort to alleviate some of the pain, I begin to read books dealing with depression.

As I read them I could see myself in some of the stories. I definitely had all of the symptoms of depression, and I knew that I had to deal with it head on if I ever wanted to get my life back on track. After reading several books I realized that I was still deeply depressed and had not really begun to deal with the issues that were causing my depression. Instinctively I knew that I needed help, and I decided that I would seek therapy.

After making the decision to get help, another series of

challenges surfaced. First of all, how was I going to find a therapist? How would I know which one to choose? What if the therapist couldn't help me? Would I be able to change? Could therapy "fix" me? What about the money to pay for it? I was completely broke and definitely couldn't pay someone to listen to my problems. What was I going to do? These were just a few of the questions that were going through my mind.

My greatest fear was wondering what would happen if my employees found out. As a manager, I was considered the leader and I definitely didn't want to appear weak in front of my co-workers. I believed that I needed to keep this a secret so that I would not lose the respect of my employees. In addition, I did not want my superiors to know because I thought I might lose my job if they found out.

After a few months of agonizing over these questions, I knew that I had to take the chance and try therapy. I didn't have any other choice. It was seek help or die - there was no gray area. I decided that I definitely wanted to live, and I somehow gained the courage to seek a therapist.

My first attempt at therapy did not go well. I walked into the therapist's office and pretended that I was seeking information for a friend. I'm sure the people there knew this was a lie, but they allowed me to walk out with some of their brochures and a phone number to their suicide hotline.

To be honest, I was absolutely terrified. But although I was scared, deep down I knew that I would have to gain the courage to try again. I waited a few days and tried a different therapist office. This time I had a completely different result.

As I walked into the office I believe the receptionist picked up on my fear. I began asking her questions about depression and whether or not they had any books that I could read. All of a sudden, a therapist walked out and began asking me questions. "May I help you?" she asked. "Not really, I'm just looking for a little information about depression." "Are you depressed?" "I'm not really sure," I answered. "Why don't you come inside and let's talk a little. Is that alright?" "I guess so."

As I followed her into her office it felt as if my heart was going to jump out of my chest. I was so nervous and afraid that I was literally dripping with sweat. She obviously picked up on this and began to put my mind at ease.

"What is your name?"

"Michael."

"Well Michael, I can sense that you are a little nervous, so let me start by asking what I can do to help you. Is there anything I can do for you?"

"Well maybe. I have been doing some research about depression and I think I'm depressed, but I'm really not sure."

"Do you feel depressed?"

"Based on what I've read so far I think I am. But to be completely honest I'm not sure I know exactly what depression is supposed to feel like. Does that make any sense to you?"

"It makes a lot of sense to me. Unfortunately, most men do not recognize how they feel. Men have been conditioned to disconnect from their emotions and that makes it extremely difficult for them to express how they really feel. Most men will tell you what they think, but they usually do not know how they feel. You apparently fit into this category."

"I'm not sure if I really understand what you're saying, but a part of me thinks that you're right."

"You just validated the point I made. You are currently speaking from an intellectual perspective, instead of an emotional one. It sounds as if you are disconnected from your emotions."

"Let's assume that you're right. If I am disconnected from my emotions, how do I get reconnected? Do you have any books on how to do this?

"Unfortunately, you cannot reconnect to your emotions by reading books. In order for you to reconnect you have to relearn how to feel. This can be accomplished through therapy with me or any trained therapist."

"I really don't understand what you mean. But if I decide to relearn how to feel how long will it take?"

"I really can't answer that question. It's really up to you and how committed you are to doing the work."

"What do you mean doing the work? What kind of work is involved?"

"In the therapeutic community, we use the word 'work' because it takes a considerable amount of effort to heal yourself so that you can reconnect with your emotions. Doing the work means that you become willing to open yourself up on an emotional level. This can be quite difficult at times."

"Well, I believe I'm ready. I'm really tired of being alone and I definitely want to experience some fun in my life again. I think I can do this, so how much will it cost?"

"I operate on a sliding scale based on your ability to pay. The most important thing is for you to make the commitment to yourself to heal and we can address the money issue at a later date. Are you ready to begin? Let's set up a date and time for you to begin your healing."

"I just wanted to thank you for being so nice and understanding. The truth is I was about to run out of your office before you showed up. Now I am really glad that I came because I really believe that you can help me."

"That is a great attitude to have. I'm glad that you trust me enough to work with you. Just remember that I can guide you, but you must be willing to do the work. As long as you believe that you can heal I can assure you that you will. Just stay committed and trust the process and you will be just fine. The truth is you have already done the hard part by showing up today. It takes an incredible amount of courage to be here and I'm proud of you for taking the first step."

~ ~ ~

As I left the therapist's office that day I knew I had just taken the biggest step of my life. I didn't know what to expect, but I knew I was willing to do whatever it took to heal my emotions and relearn how to feel. I became committed to my own healing, and I can now say that I'm emotionally healed and connected to my authentic self.

As the therapist mentioned, it wasn't easy, but it was definitely possible. It has been one of the most challenging, yet most fulfilling, journeys of my life.

I cannot put into words the joy I feel on a regular basis as a result of carrying out my emotional work. My relationships now work, my creativity and sense of reverence are enhanced, my love of nature has been rekindled, and my professional life is rewarding and fulfilling. I took the road less traveled and it has made all the difference in the world for me.

I wanted to share this story because there is such a negative stigma about men and therapy that I believe it's time for a new conversation. In this new conversation, men will recognize the importance of healing their emotions and they will put forth the effort to do their healing work.

When we learn to support each other in our growth we can remove the fear and stigma of being emotionally vulnerable, which will ultimately result in us being happier human beings. I personally believe this is the most important work that men can participate in, and we must begin supporting each other through this process.

If we gain the courage to do this work, we will see a decline in domestic violence, child abuse, alcoholism, and random acts of violence. The time has come for a new conversation about our emotional healing.

Are you willing to join in the conversation?

So, the first step in making peace with your past is to make sure you do some emotional healing work. It may be in the form of therapy, but it could also be through support groups like AA. The key is to become 100% committed to healing your heart and making peace with your past. Once you commit and then take action I can assure you that you will begin to feel better about your life, and it will definitely get easier. It won't be an easy process, but I promise you it will be worth it.

2. Workshops/Seminars/Webinars

The second thing I recommend you do is to be willing to participate in personal development seminars. If you have never done anything like this before, you're simply going to have to trust me. There are countless seminars available that can support you in making peace with your past. There are one-day seminars, three-day retreats, online webinars, and a wide variety of others that can assist you along your journey. Here are just a few I have found extremely helpful.

Landmark Education is a powerful personal development seminar that can support you in making tremendous leaps in your life. It is a deep immersion into your limiting beliefs that may be holding you back and it provides you with tools and support to empower you to take complete control of your life. www.landmarkeducation.com.

If you are male, I highly recommend a three-day workshop

called The New Warrior Training Adventure. It is carried out by an organization called The Mankind Project, and without question, it is one of the most transformational experiences you will ever encounter. One of the benefits of doing this training is the ongoing support you receive after it is completed. Through regular meetings called I-Groups, participants continue their healing and transformation and develop connections and bonds with men that help them integrate the things they learned in the trainings into their lives at a much deeper level.

You can find them at: **mankindproject.org.**

If you are female, they have a sister organization called The Woman Within, who offer similar training.

You can find them at: **womanwithin.org.**

There are several organizations offers inner-child healing workshops around the country. I suggest you search online for inner child work and find a resource in your area. You will simply have to trust yourself and find one that feels right for you.

Nothing is more important in healing and transformation than being engaged with other human beings. Creating intimacy and vulnerability can't come from reading a book, so I highly recommend you participate in a workshop or seminar setting. However, you can begin the process by reading some books by John Bradshaw if you aren't comfortable attending the workshops. Two of my favorites are *Healing the Shame That Binds You* and *Homecoming*. I highly recommend you pick up a copy of both.

The key is to become 100% committed to making peace with your past. You have to want it more than anything. You have to listen to that still small voice within you calling you to do this work. It's all up to you!

I am absolutely convinced that making peace with your past is a surefire way to achieve true freedom and happiness. As I've mentioned before, it won't be easy, but it will definitely be worth it. If you commit to doing this I can promise you that you will experience deep inner peace, less anxiety, no more depression, a deeper sense of passion and purpose, and a deep inner knowing that you can create the life of your dreams. This is the foundation for being a great entrepreneur; removing the internal obstacles that can sabotage your success and keep you from being genuinely happy with your business and your life.

Isn't that what you really want - a more rewarding and fulfilling life experience? If the answer is yes, begin by making peace with your past and I can assure you that you will have everything you need to become the best entrepreneur you can possibly be.

With that being said, I want to touch on the subject of personal relationships. One of the biggest mistakes I made in my first marriage was choosing someone who didn't share the same ambition as me. She believed I should have been happy with my nice, secure corporate position and she completely disagreed with me trying to become an entrepreneur. This caused a lot of friction in our marriage and in some ways, it actually led to our divorce.

As I reflect back on that marriage I have taken complete

responsibility for my part in the divorce and I have no regrets about our decision to separate. What I learned was I needed to find someone who understood my drive and dreams of being an entrepreneur. I needed a woman who had faith in my abilities and me and would support my dreams. Someone who I could trust to be by my side as I built my business and someone who would be my life partner physically, emotionally, spiritually, and financially.

As a result of doing my inner work and removing a lot of emotional baggage, I was able to find a woman who was absolutely perfect for me. We have been happily married for 16 years now and she is the absolute love of my life. My marriage takes priority over my business. I now realize that the most important thing in life is to have someone to love and share life with and fortunately for me I now have the right partner. I make sure I never take her for granted and I constantly nurture our relationship by being emotionally available and giving her lots of attention, appreciation, and affection.

As entrepreneurs, it's easy to get lost in our businesses and neglect the things which are truly important like faith, family, and friends. Don't make that mistake. Make relationships a high priority in your life because they really are the glue that holds your life together.

*"Making money isn't hard in itself...
What's hard is to earn it doing something
worth devoting one's life to."*

Carlos Ruiz Zafón

Chapter 6
It's Not About the Money

It's been said: "When you do what you love the money will follow." Which, from a spiritual perspective, is absolutely true, but from a practical business perspective it is an incomplete teaching. Let's modify it just a bit. When you do what you love and learn to market and promote your business, then the money will follow.

The problem with combining spiritual teachings with building a business is that too many spiritual people are unwilling to take action. One of the reasons why this is a big problem can be traced back to a movie called The Secret. The Secret is a 2006 film consisting of a series of interviews designed to demonstrate the New Thought claim that everything one wants or needs can be satisfied by believing in an outcome, repeatedly thinking about it, and maintaining positive emotional states to "attract" the desired outcome. In other words, the movie promoted the idea that all you had to do was believe, think and feel deeply about a thing and you could manifest that thing into your life without really taking any action. The implication was that you "attract" things into your life without any physical effort.

As I see it, the problem is they didn't mention how difficult and challenging it is and how, without actual action, you will not manifest your desires. Manifesting your desires and using the Law of Attraction is a lot more than just sitting around praying, visualizing, and believing things are going to just show up for you.

But let me be clear: I fervently and passionately believe in the Law of Attraction. That is the reason I've mentioned it several times throughout this book. But my experience has taught me that you must first pray and then move your feet. This is why even the good book says: "Faith without works is dead."

A more appropriate quote that pertains to the chapter title "It's Not About the Money" would be: "When you do what you love, you never have to work a day in your life." This is what this chapter is about. It's about discovering the things that you love to do and maybe even figuring out a way to make a business out of it.

When you think of the word *creativity* what comes to mind? Do you think about artists? Photographers? Graphic Designers? Musicians?

One definition of creativity is: "a phenomenon whereby something new and somehow valuable is formed. The created item may be intangible (such as an idea, a scientific theory, a musical composition, or a joke) or a physical object (such as an invention, a literary work, or a painting)." Another definition is: "the use of the imagination or original ideas, especially in the production of an artistic work."

Based on these descriptions, where do you think creativity comes from? Does creativity come from the brain? Is it genetic and passed down through our DNA? Is it something we pick up based on the culture and society we come from?

What do you think?

The next question could be, is everyone creative? Or is creativity limited to a select few? So, let me answer the latter question first. I believe every human being is creative. Creativity is a gift that everyone receives. Unfortunately, very few people recognize and express their gifts and that is one of the great tragedies of being human.

For the former question, I believe creativity comes from the Source or Infinite intelligence. Creativity is not a function of the brain or the intellect, it is an expression of the Infinite Intelligence that created the Universe. Put another way, creativity comes from your heart, not your head. In this case, your heart is actually your Soul.

In his groundbreaking New York Times bestselling book, *The Seat of The Soul*, Gary Zukav introduced a profound theory that suggested human beings were actually still evolving. His theory is that human beings are evolving from what he called "five sensory beings to multisensory beings". As human beings, we have been taught to believe that we only have five senses. Seeing, hearing, tasting, touching, and smelling. In his theory, he suggests not only do we have a sixth sense, which would include intuition, but we also have the capacity to have a multiplicity of senses that connect us to Infinite Intelligence.

I definitely believe in his theory and this is why I believe everyone is creative. Think of it this way. Imagine a portable radio. The radio has multiple channels that receive multiple signals, but each channel is separate and distinct from the other channels. Each channel represents a human being. Although there are multiple signals coming into the radio, they all originate from the same source, which is Infinite Intelligence. So, each human being is tuned in to a separate frequency or vibration.

Currently, there are approximately 7.6 billion people on earth, which means there are 7.6 billion stations on the Universal radio. Each one is separate and has its own unique vibration. When we learn to tune in to our unique frequency we gain access to our unique creativity.

Here is a quote from the inventor of the telephone, Alexander Graham Bell, which substantiates my belief in the Universal Radio.

> "It has occurred to me that there must be a great deal to be learned about the effect of those vibrations in the great gap, where the ordinary human senses are unable to hear, see, or feel the movement... It seems to me that in this gap lie the vibrations that we have assumed to be given off by our brains and nerve cells when we think. We may assume that the brain cells act as a battery and that the current produced, flows along the nerves. But does it end there? Does it not pass out of the body in waves that flow around the world unperceived by our senses, just as wireless (radio)

waves passed unperceived before Hertz and others discovered their existence?"

Graham also had some fascinating statements regarding this concept. Here are just a few of his thoughts:

1. The brain is both a broadcaster and a receiver.
2. You can send and receive better under the influence of emotion.
3. The thoughts you send are those that you want to burn into your subconscious.
4. The thoughts you receive appear in your creative imagination.
5. Your subconscious mind is both a storehouse of information and the way you connect with Infinite Intelligence.
6. Because everything in the universe is a part of the same basic energy, the energy of your subconscious mind shares a connection with the energy of other subconscious minds.
7. Under certain circumstances, the energy of an idea that is outside your mind can, through Infinite Intelligence, become a part of your subconscious mind.
8. When such ideas come to you, they flash into your creative imagination as hunches, intuitions, flashes of insight, or inspirations.

Fascinating, don't you think?

One of the Universal laws I mentioned was the Universe is Infinite. Using the Universal radio analogy, Infinite Intelligence has an infinite supply of creativity and creative ideas that it streams to human beings. As such, you as a human being have an infinite capacity for creativity.

Some of you reading this may be thinking to yourself that you aren't creative. Rest assured that nothing could be further from the truth. If you are a human being reading these words I can assure you that you are creative. Creativity is your birthright; however, you may have simply disconnected from your creative self. So how and why did you do that? you may be asking. Let me explain.

Remember when you were a little kid and you used your imagination to create things? Maybe you pretended to be a fireman or a racecar driver. Maybe you pretended to be a doctor or a lawyer. Try to recall an experience where you pretended to be something that you wanted to be when you grew up.

In your imagination, you would literally become the thing you were imagining. You could not distinguish reality from make-believe because in your creative mind it was very real.

For me, I always dreamed of being an entrepreneur. Although I had no idea what that word meant when I was a kid I intuitively knew that was what I wanted to be when I grew up. As mentioned in an earlier chapter, when I was a kid I would pretend to be an entrepreneur and I would role play negotiations with businessmen who were very rich. I remember some of the dialogs I had with myself as I pretended to be two different businessmen competing for million-dollar deals.

As children, our minds and hearts are wide open to

imagination and creativity. In some ways, you could say we bypass our intellects and connect with our hearts, which is the connection to Infinite Intelligence, which is the source of all creativity.

As we grow older, we stop listening to our hearts and begin paying more attention to our rational minds. We are taught to think rationally and logically. Our culture and society then begins to ridicule us for dreaming and using our imaginations and eventually we simply lose touch with our connection to our imagination. In other words, we tune out from the Universal radio frequency that connects us to the Source. In essence, we turn off the Universal radio.

Once again, I refer back to the importance of spiritual compensation. Creativity and imagination are spiritual tools that come from the Source. Imagination is simply the "imaging in" of divine ideas and since ideas are the currency of the Universe, if we disconnect from the Source we lose our creativity. By focusing on spiritual compensation, it opens up the channel and turns the Universal radio back on.

The Universal Radio is always broadcasting. It cannot be turned off. It is always sending out signals to anyone who is willing to tune in. Your challenge is to tune in to your unique station and frequency and tap into your creativity.

If you're struggling with this concept, then let's look at some ways to help you.

The key to tapping into your creativity is to get in touch with your feelings. Feelings are the language of the Soul and without them, you cannot access your creativity. As mentioned in an earlier chapter, the most direct way to do this is to make peace with your past - which means you become willing to heal any emotional pain or trauma that you may be carrying from your childhood. Doing your inner emotional work is without a doubt the most important component in gaining access to your creativity. All negative emotions like anger, shame, hatred, resentment, anxiety, and guilt actually block the flow of creativity. By healing these negative emotions, you clear the channel for the Universal radio to send you divine ideas and creativity.

Once you've healed your emotions, the most powerful way to stay connected to the Universal radio is through meditation. Meditation isn't about making your mind go blank and thinking about nothing, it's the practice of being mindful and aware of what you are thinking. It is a practice of simply being aware. It is noticing your thoughts and your feelings and being able to recognize what the source is of those thoughts and feelings.

When you take ownership of your feelings and understand that you actually control your feelings and your thoughts, you become the master of your life and your destiny. To do so you must remember this quote; "if you do not go within, you will always go without." Every major religion points to this simple idea. There is divinity inside you and you are responsible for accessing it. Here is another powerful quote to contemplate. "If an egg is broken from the outside, life ends. If it is broken from the inside, life begins." Always begin from within!

The big challenge for you as an entrepreneur is to not focus on things outside of yourself. In other words, do not make financial compensation your primary focus. We are constantly bombarded with images of wealth, with things like money, cars, mansions, jets, and diamonds but true wealth actually comes from within. True wealth is having inner peace, dynamic health, great relationships and financial abundance. When you can balance these four things in your life then you are truly wealthy.

Let me say this again: there is absolutely nothing wrong with financial compensation. As a matter of fact, I want you to dream big and make creating financial wealth a high priority. Just make sure it isn't your first priority.

If we make financial compensation our primary goal it can actually keep us from accessing our creativity. Let me share a story from my own life to make a point.

I used to be driven by financial compensation. I dreamed about having big mansions and fancy cars and lots of money in the bank. I, therefore, chased money and made it my highest priority. At the time, I had no idea what spiritual compensation was because I was actually an atheist. I believed if I worked really hard, set goals for myself, and became an entrepreneur, I would eventually become rich and be happy. So, I spent a lot of time, energy, and effort trying to figure out how to get rich. I read get-rich-quick books, attended get-rich-quick seminars, joined multi-level marketing companies, started a real estate company, started a telephone phone booth building company, and even started a video production company for real estate agents. I also started a customer service training and consulting company in my attempt to get rich. However, each of these businesses failed for a wide variety of reasons, but primarily because I was chasing money instead of finding my purpose (which is spiritual).

When I finally focused my attention on spiritual compensation and gained a connection to the Universal Radio, everything changed for me. I then tapped into my creativity (which I didn't even know I had) and discovered that I have the gift of writing and communicating. I then became an author and motivational speaker, which led me to create my own publishing company. Amazingly, I never dreamed of being a writer or a speaker. I have no formal training or special degrees; I simply taught myself how to write and challenged myself to become a great speaker. All I know is that I've always dreamed of being an entrepreneur, and as a result of tapping into Infinite Intelligence I've found the business I was destined to create.

I have now written seven books (with three more already in the works), created, produced, and hosted a cable television show and received numerous awards as a motivational speaker.

I share my story because I am absolutely convinced that you have access to the Universal Radio. It is up to you to make that connection and tap into your creativity. Once you do, it will guide you to find the right outlet for your creativity. Maybe it's a business or maybe it's not, but your goal should simply be to make the connection and find out for yourself.

If you choose to make the connection, I can assure you that you will have an infinite supply of creativity. As a matter of fact, you may find it difficult to contain it all. I am blown away by the amount of creativity I have now that I've connected to the Universal Radio. It's actually a miracle how it works. Whenever I'm writing a new book I simply tune in to my direct channel on the radio and I literally just download the book. It is an amazing process that is difficult to describe, but in essence, I simply take dictation of the words that are flowing through me. At times I can't even keep up with the downloads. Pages and pages of insights just pour through me and I simply capture them on my computer.

This is what happens for all creative people. If you've ever watched a painter or artist create beautiful works of art, it's the same process. They are simply tuning in to their specific channel and Infinite Intelligence is sending them downloads. Some people use the term "manifesting" which is another way of saying downloading. Manifesting is the process of bringing something from the invisible to the visible. It's bringing something from the spiritual to the physical.

Believe it or not, you have this same ability. Once again, it's up to you to access it.

I shared this quote at the beginning of this chapter; "when you do what you love, you'll never work a day in your life." This is the beauty and the gift of creativity. As a writer and publisher, I actually don't consider writing as work. It's actually fun for me. I love writing books and it has nothing to do with making money. Although I receive compensation for my "work" I would still do it even if I didn't earn a dime. I do it because I love to, and it brings me an infinite amount of joy and satisfaction.

This should be your goal as well. You should seek to find the things you love to do and then figure out a way to be compensated for doing what you love.

So, would you like me to share how you know when you're doing what you love? I'd be glad to!

There are three ways to know if you are doing what you truly love.

1. You do it without the thought of compensation. When you truly love to do something you never think about getting paid to do it. This does not mean that you can't get paid, it means that getting paid isn't important. You do it because it brings you joy and lights you up. Just being able to do it is compensation enough.

So, ask yourself right now, *what is something you love to do?*

2. When you are doing what you love time literally disappears. Albert Einstein once said, "If you're on a porch kissing a pretty girl, one hour feels like one minute. But if you put your hand on a hot stove, one minute feels like one hour. This is relativity."

When you are doing what you love time stands still. As a

writer, I can be at my computer for ten hours and I promise you it feels like ten minutes. When I get into a creative flow I lose all track of time. Have you ever had the experience of losing track of time while doing something you love?

3. When you are doing what you love you want to share it with others. Whenever we are being creative, there is a part of us that wants to share our creations with others. Whether it's a piece of art, a book, a song, or a photograph we receive joy by bringing joy to others.

What have you created you would like to share with others?

When it's all said and done, as an entrepreneur it isn't always about the money. It's really about creative expression and finding ways to be compensated for that expression. Yes, if you want to start and run a business you must make money to keep your business open, but I hope this chapter has shed some light on the fact that receiving spiritual compensation and being connected to Infinite Intelligence is a surefire way to creating authentic wealth and a successful business.

"It's not how much money you make, but how much money you keep, how hard it works for you, and how many generations you keep it for."

Robert Kiyosaki

Chapter 7

It's All About the Money

When it comes to starting a business, few things are as difficult as locating funding to get started. Raising capital can be a pure pain in the butt for any entrepreneur. But what if it didn't have to be so difficult? What if there was a spiritual solution to the problem of locating funding?

Throughout this book, I've talked about the Infinite Intelligence that created the Universe, and I've mentioned we all have access to this Infinite Intelligence. In the last chapter, I talked about creativity, so what if there are *creative* solutions to finding funding?

I believe there are, so I would like to share a few lessons I've learned about receiving funding. First of all, it's important you understand the power of belief. Belief can be defined as *"trust, faith or confidence in someone or something."* The first lesson you must learn is your belief in your ability to find funding is going to govern whether or not you actually find it.

To increase your chance of locating funding, the first thing you must do is examine your beliefs about money. This is absolutely critical. Your deeply held beliefs about money will impact your ability to find it and keep it.

I am going to share some wisdom from a man named T. Harv Eker. He is the author of the New York Times best-selling book, *Secrets of The Millionaire Mind.*

"Having the right set of beliefs that support your success and financial freedom is critical to achieving your life's desires. But most people have non-supportive, fear-based beliefs about money, wealth and success that were developed by modeling influencers like parents, friends, teachers, the media and even the web.

The good news is that beliefs are neither right nor wrong – they are only beliefs – which means you can change them if you want to. If a belief is not helping you, simply replace it with one that does."

This is your key to unlocking the door to funding. You must first challenge your deeply held beliefs about money and if they aren't serving you, then you must be willing to change them.

So, I'm going to list 10 fear-based beliefs T. Harv Eker shared and a lot of people believe and hold on to. As long as you're holding on to these beliefs it will impact your ability to bring money into your life. So, take a moment to read this list and see if you're holding on to any of these fear-based beliefs.

1. I have to work hard for money
2. Money is a limited resource
3. I can't control if I become wealthy or not
4. It takes a lot of money to start a business
5. Money can't buy me happiness

6. More money means more problems

7. Money is the root of all evil

8. I never have any extra money

9. I can either make money or do what I love, not both

10. It's not right to be rich when so many other people are poor

Now, I want you to be completely honest with yourself and underline the beliefs from this list you may have been holding on to. The key to changing any belief is to first acknowledge you have it. So, go ahead and underline any of the fear-based beliefs you may have.

And now I want you to read this list of millionaire beliefs and then replace the fear-based ones with these.

1. I do what I love, I solve problems, and I make a large profit

2. There's enough money for everyone who is willing to earn it

3. I create my life and take consistent actions to make it how I want it

4. Starting my own business will allow me to have no limits on my income

5. Money gives me the freedom to do things to improve my quality of life

6. More money means more choices in every aspect of my life

7. Money is a resource to do good in my life and for others

8. I manage my money because when I do, more

money comes my way

9. I don't have to choose between making money and pursuing my passion. I can do both

10. I can do more for others when I'm rich than when I'm broke

Changing deeply held beliefs can be challenging, but rest assured you *can* do it. One way to do it is by using the Mirror Technique. Simply stand in front of a mirror and repeat each millionaire belief out loud to yourself. It's important you pay attention to how you feel as you say them to ensure you change them. As you say them, simply notice how you feel. If you feel a little timid at first that's okay. But make sure you get to a point where you are not only comfortable saying them, but you also have a deep conviction that they are true for you. It might take several attempts to change them, but you will feel a shift inside yourself when the belief changes. Do this on a regular basis and I can assure you your attitude and your flow of money will change.

Once you identify your fear-based beliefs and change them, then you must learn to pay attention to the synchronistic events that will start to occur. This is based on spiritual principles and at the beginning might feel a little irrational. It's important you learn to trust Infinite Intelligence and trust has nothing to do with what you think - it has everything to do with how you feel. This is why it's so important to trust your inner wisdom. As Master Yoda so succinctly stated, "You must feel The Force." I'll say this again: having faith and trusting the Universe has very little to do with what you think. It has everything to do with how you feel. Knowing is a feeling. It is the complete absence of doubt. You may not fully understand it, but intuitively you must learn to trust it.

I want to share an experience to substantiate what I mean.

During the darkest period of my life, I was completely broke and was living in a run-down dilapidated building with no electricity. I had a bicycle for transportation and I didn't have a job. In order to eat, I would sell blood plasma to get money. One day I went to church and the minister was preaching about trust. He said every adversity was designed to help us build unshakable faith and complete trust that the Universe had our backs.

After the sermon, I was thinking about what he said, and I made an internal decision that I was going to completely surrender and trust the Universe. As I was riding my bike home I came to an intersection where a homeless man asking for money. I had exactly 2 dollars to my name and I didn't have any food at home. But a part of me said I trust the Universe to be my financial supply, and I gave the homeless man my last 2 dollars.

As he thanked me for my generosity a part of me inside lit up like a Christmas tree. I can't fully explain the feeling, but there were knowingness and a trust I had never felt before. I intuitively knew that everything was going to work out.

When I got home I was pleasantly surprised to see a friend of mine whom I hadn't seen in a couple of years. He and I had met in Austin, Texas, and I never told him I was moving to Houston. I hadn't given my address to anyone because the room I was renting didn't really have an address. I didn't have a phone or a forwarding address, so how did he find me? It turns out he had been looking for me for approximately three weeks. He was getting ready to leave the country and he wanted to see me before he left.

Amazingly, he received a lead from someone who attended the church I went to and miraculously he had found me. He invited me to dinner and we went out to eat and had a wonderful time catching up. He and I both attended the same church and held the same beliefs about God and the Universe, so I shared the story with him about the sermon and trusting the Universe and how I recognized how the Universe was supporting me by him paying for dinner. We both laughed and acknowledged the amazing synchronicities that brought us back together.

After a couple of hours, it was time for him to go. As he was getting ready to leave, he hugged me and then stuck out his hand and said he wanted to give me a gift. He then handed me a fifty-dollar bill and said: "The Universe wants you to have this." I immediately broke down in tears. They were tears of joy because I recognized how all the synchronicities had led up to that very moment and the Universe was saying; this is your gift for trusting me. Know that I always have your back.

Experiences like this continue to happen to me all the time. They are not rational or logical. There are countless miracles that have occurred which cannot be explained. As I look back over my life and all the adversities I've had to overcome, I am filled with a deep sense of gratitude and awe of this amazing Universe we live in.

You too can experience these types of miracles if you're open to them, but it begins with developing a deep level of trust with the Universe.

As mentioned earlier, you must be willing to take action to apply the law of attraction. Funding will not fall from the sky, but it can come from unsuspected places. So, make sure you begin with traditional methods of securing funding. Start with family and friends by enrolling them in your vision and providing them with a solid plan for using the money and paying it back. If possible, using credit cards can also be an option and last but not least, you can approach your financial institutions like your bank or credit union.

Truth be told there are more funding options for entrepreneurs than ever before. Although I place all my faith in the Universe (and my hope is you learn to do the same), I also take logical and rational approaches to locating funding.

I want to close this chapter with a few ideas from Peter Diamandis. He highlights why there is a global abundance of capital and why you should be optimistic about locating funding for your venture. He mentions there are four different funding sources every entrepreneur should know.

1. Crowdfunding
2. Venture funding
3. Initial coin offerings (ICOs)
4. Sovereign wealth funds and mega funds

Let's dive in...

The Rise of Crowdfunding

At the low end of capital abundance is crowdfunding, a peer-to-peer network where anyone can present their product or service to the world and ask for funding.

Funding can come in the form of a loan, an equity investment, a reward, or an advanced purchase of the proposed product or service.

The total worldwide volume of crowdfunding, inclusive of peer-to-peer lending, was $34 billion in 2017, with 375 crowdfunding platforms in North America alone. But this too, like many digital platforms, is experiencing double-digit growth. Experts project crowdfunding to reach $300 billion by 2025.

Kickstarter, one of the most popular reward-based crowdsourcing platforms, has launched almost 400,000 projects, and over $3 billion has been pledged on the site.

The most successful Kickstarter to date, Pebble Time, raised just over $20 million in only 37 days.

Ultimately, crowdfunding fully *democratizes* access to capital, allowing anyone with a good idea, anywhere, to get the cash they need to get going.

No surprise that Goldman Sachs described crowdfunding as "potentially the most disruptive of all the new models of finance."

Venture Funding

In contrast, venture funding has been a more traditional source of startup capital over the past five decades, helping to birth household names from Apple and Google to Amazon and Uber.

Venture capitalists, better known as VCs, raise money from individuals, corporations, and institutional investors (e.g. pension funds) and invest that money in exchange for equity into high-growth companies.

Depending on the stage of the company and the size of the fund, these investments range widely, from a hundred thousand dollars during a seed stage to hundreds of millions of dollars to support later growth-stage companies.

Here again, the world is experiencing staggering global growth. In 2017, we saw new records set in venture investing:

- In the U.S. venture investments reached $84 billion
- In Asia venture peaked at $48 billion
- European venture reached a new all-time high of $19.1 billion

Cryptocurrencies & ICOs

New to the scene of capital formation is the "Initial Coin Offering," or ICO, a new fundraising tool emerging out of the cryptocurrency - blockchain realm.

An ICO is a way to crowdfund your business venture by

issuing your own tokens that can then be used to redeem value in the ecosystem of your startup.

In some cases, the tokens have a clear utility in a company, for example, they may be used to vote in a prediction marketplace.

In other cases, they may be used as security -- they may represent a fractional share of a piece of real estate listed on the blockchain.

If you do a good job selling your vision, people will buy those tokens and you'll end up with the capital you need to start your venture.

A lot of these tokens (coins) can also be traded on major cryptocurrency exchanges. That means if your project goes well, your tokens will rise in value and investors will be able to sell them for a nice profit.

Perhaps best of all, for the entrepreneur, the capital that comes in via an ICO is non-dilutive, meaning you give investors no equity -- for instance, no ownership and no control -- in your company, no matter how much your ICO might raise.

ICOs are still highly controversial, though. Their unregulated nature means scammers have plenty of opportunities to line their pockets.

According to the Wall Street Journal, the total amount invested in ICOs has risen from $6.6 billion in 2017 to $7.15 billion USD in the first half of 2018 -- despite regulatory uncertainty and restrictions in many major countries, such as China and South Korea.

ICOs are famous for raising money fast and in vast amounts. There are hundreds of examples that will make your head spin, and make you wonder why you haven't already launched your own ICO.

The number of ICOs per quarter has also ballooned, from roughly a dozen in Q1 of 2017 to over 100 in Q4 of 2017.

Sovereigns and the Vision Fund

When it comes to the motherlode of deployable capital, look no further than Sovereign Wealth Funds (SWFs), which hold an estimated $6.59 *trillion* in assets.

As the promise and economic potential of exponential startups continue to climb, it's no surprise that SWFs are lining up to invest in the tech startup world searching to yield outsized returns.

Globally, in 2017, there were 42 SWF deals valued at some $16.2 billion last year, according to the Sovereign Wealth Lab research center at Madrid's IE Business School.

But this $16.2 billion pales in comparison with the passion and checkbook of Masayoshi Son's mega fund, the "Vision Fund," an initial $100 billion which he hopes to grow tenfold in the decade ahead.

Why raise such an enormous fund? "I totally believe this concept," he said, of the Singularity. "In next 30 years, this will become a reality. I truly believe it's coming, that's why

I'm in a hurry – to aggregate the cash, to invest."

And aggregate the cash he has done.

The Vision Fund had its start in September 2016 when Mohammed bin Salman, then deputy crown prince of Saudi Arabia, flew to Tokyo in search of mechanisms to diversify his country's oil-dominated future.

There he met with Son, who pitched him the idea of setting up the largest investment fund in history to finance technology startups.

In less than an hour, bin Salman agreed to become the cornerstone investor.

"Forty-five minutes, $45 billion," Son later said on the David Rubenstein Show. "One billion dollars per minute."

Quickly thereafter, other LPs like the UAE-based Mubadala Investment Company and private companies like Apple, Foxconn, and Qualcomm joined in.

Softbank, largely a one-man show when it comes to deals, made about 100 investments in the first year, worth $36 billion, which is more in dollar terms than Silicon Valley's top two heavyweights, Sequoia Capital and Silver Lake, combined.

Perhaps even more exciting in our abundance of capital thesis are Masa Son's plans to increase his vision fund by ten times.

The $100 Billion Vision Fund is just "the first step,"

according to Son, who said he is already working to establish a second Vision Fund in the next two or three years.

"We will briskly expand the scale," he told Nikkei. "Vision Funds 2, 3, and 4 will be established every two to three years."

"We are creating a mechanism to increase our funding ability from 10 trillion yen to 20 trillion yen to 100 trillion yen," Son said. 100 trillion yen equals roughly $880 billion based on current currency rates.

Son said that SoftBank plans to invest in at least 1,000 tech companies in areas like artificial intelligence and robotics over the next 10 years. SoftBank has already invested in a wide range of companies this year, including Brain Corp, Mailbox, Boston Dynamics, Improbable, Nvidia, Slack, WeWork, OneWeb, Didi, and Uber.

Final Thoughts...

For entrepreneurs, this is an exciting time.

Between crowdfunding sites, ICOs, and SWFs, there is no capital-related excuse to put off pursuing your MTP and Moonshot.

The speed at which we can go from "I've got an idea" to "I run a billion-dollar company" is moving faster than ever.

~~~

Peter's insights fill me with optimism and excitement for

the future. As mentioned, never before has it been simpler to become an entrepreneur. These resources to capital should also excite you. It's important you learn about them in case you are looking for ways to launch your business. Remember, the Universe is infinite and there is an infinite amount of ways for you to fund your company. Be open to all opportunities and when that door opens run through it as fast as you can.

"It's always a little bit frustrating to me when people have a negative relationship with failure. Failure is a massive part of being able to be successful. You have to get comfortable with failure. Failure is where all of the lessons are."

Will Smith

Chapter 8

There Is No Such Thing As Failure

In 1983 I was living the American Dream. I was twenty-three years old, I was married, I had purchased my first home, I had two wonderful children, had great credit, and was able to take nice vacations. By society's standards, I was pretty successful. On the outside, it looked as if I had the perfect life and if you asked any of my friends about me they would have told you I had it all together.

But internally something was wrong. I couldn't explain it, and I definitely didn't understand it, but somehow, I felt I was living a lie. I felt as if I were wearing a mask and pretending to be someone I wasn't. I felt as if I were trapped on a roller coaster I couldn't get off. I was going round and round and up and down, but I really wasn't going anywhere. I was feeling stuck.

In 1989 my American Dream turned into the American Nightmare as I experienced divorce, bankruptcy, foreclosure, and a deep state of depression. I was dumbfounded! How in the world had my perfect American Dream collapsed so fast and ended up so devastating? What the hell happened?

I had failed and failed miserably. My life was in total chaos and I couldn't see a way out. What was I going to do? How was I going to get out of this mess?

After a couple of years, things got worse. I lost my job, my car was repossessed, and I was on the verge of being homeless. Things were looking pretty bad. I had fallen into a deep state of depression and I couldn't see a way to dig myself out of the deep hole I was in.

During the darkest period of my life, at a time when I was considering giving up, I received a miracle. I was sitting up late one night because I was too depressed to sleep. I was sitting at the edge of my bed staring across the room at my bookshelf. I happened to notice every book on my bookshelf had something to do with getting rich and making money. As I sat there staring at the books, all of a sudden, I heard a bodiless voice whisper this question into my mind; *"Michael, what if you took all the energy and effort you've used in trying to get rich and simply figure out how to be happy?"*

There is no way to describe the feeling I got after hearing that question. Something in me shifted. I can't explain it, but all of a sudden, my depression lifted, and I had a deep sense of clarity that everything was going to be okay. All of a sudden, I begin to smile, which I hadn't done in a very long time. As a result of that single question, my life changed in an instant. I knew exactly what I needed to do. I needed to figure out how to be happy again. I needed to get back the joy and passion I remembered feeling as a child and no matter what it took I was committed to putting my life back together.

This miracle is what turned my life around. From that point

on I stopped reading books on getting rich and making money. I started reading books on philosophy and psychology, metaphysics and spirituality, personal development and motivation. This began my "journey of transformation", which helped me turn my life around and eventually create the life I've always dreamed of.

Here is a poem I wrote describing my feelings of being trapped on the rollercoaster, in which I eventually figured out how to get off.

The Roller Coaster

I had heard a lot about the rollercoaster. Initially, I didn't want to go and see it, but everyone kept saying, "You have to check it out and get on it. It will be so much fun."

Reluctantly, I went to see it. It was intriguing and enticing and it looked like fun.

"You have to get on it!" everyone said.
"I'm not sure that I want to."
"But everyone loves getting on the Rollercoaster," they said.
"I don't think I'll like it."
"Go ahead and try it, you'll like it," everyone said.

So, I tried it.

At the beginning it was fun. Going round and round and up and down with friends who also seemed to be having fun was initially enjoyable.

But after a short while, I got bored and tired. I didn't want to ride it any more. I decided that I wanted to get off.

"You can't get off," everyone said.
"But I'm ready to."
"No one gets off the rollercoaster once they get on."
"Why not?"
"They just don't."
"But I'm ready to get off."
"Why not ride it a little longer and see if you'll change your mind?" they said.
"Okay, I'll try it a little longer."

Round and round, up and down I went pretending that I was enjoying myself.

But after a while, I began to get angry. I was tired of the rollercoaster and I realized I shouldn't have got on it in the first place. I wanted to get off, but I didn't know how.

"I'm really sick of this rollercoaster. I want to get off right now."
"We're sorry but you must stay on the rollercoaster. That's the rule."
"Well, I guess I'm going to have to break the rule because I'm about to get off."
"But if you break the rule no one will like you and you will probably get hurt," they said.
"I don't care about anyone else. I want to get off now. Who can I talk to about getting off this thing?"
"No one knows how to get off," they said.
"I'm sure someone knows, I just have to find them."
"It's been said that only a few people have ever got off this rollercoaster. And no one really knows what happened

to them. Some believe that people have even been killed trying to get off. Why take that risk?"

"At this point, I'm willing to take that risk. I don't care what people think or what people are going to say. I refuse to keep going round and round and getting nowhere on this thing, and I must do something to get off."

I didn't know what to do, but I knew that I couldn't stay on the rollercoaster. I needed a plan and I needed it soon. I felt as though I was dying, and I really wanted to live again.

But what about the risk? What if what they say is true? What if I really can't get off or what if I get killed trying to get off?

At this point, I decide I have only one choice. And that choice is to live. I don't know what is going to happen, but I know if I stay on this thing I'm already dead. I have to trust my inner instincts and take the chance and simply jump off. I'm not sure where I'll land or if I'll get hurt or even die, but I just know that I have to jump.

So, despite what everyone else was saying and the fear and uncertainty I felt, I took a deep breath and jumped. As my body was hurled through the air uncontrollably, surprisingly I felt a deep sense of calm and inner peace, and then I did exactly what I intuitively knew I could do - I flew!

Can you relate?

~ ~ ~

Throughout this book, I've mentioned my belief in the

Infinite Intelligence that created this Universe and how each of us as human beings have direct access to this Intelligence. I have come to know that the bodiless voice I heard asking me to figure out how to be happy was the voice of this Intelligence. Some people refer to it as your Higher Self or Authentic Self, but I simply refer to it as The Source.

As a result of my belief in, and connection to, this Source, I can now see in retrospect how every adversity I've ever experienced brought me a gift and a lesson for my highest good. No matter how difficult or painful the lesson may have been, it ultimately taught me something about myself that has allowed me to become a better human being. If I had a chance to do my life all over again I wouldn't change a thing because in retrospect I now see how every experience, no matter how difficult or painful, helped me become the man I am today.

It is my absolute conviction there is but one presence and one power in the Universe and that power is love and that power is good. I am absolutely convinced this love can only do one thing and that's to love us. I don't believe there's an opposing force or evil entity working against or opposed to this loving presence. Whenever we experience pain or suffering it isn't that we're being punished, we're simply being redirected to something better than what we are experiencing. The only time we experience suffering is when we believe we are separate from and disconnected from the Source. When we open our hearts and our minds to this divine truth we become masters of our own destiny and the captain of our own ship.

With that thought in mind, I want to talk about something that keeps a lot of entrepreneurs from succeeding in business and in life. It is the topic of failure and it's important for you to face this topic head on.

Fear of failure can be a powerful driving force in the life of an entrepreneur. For some people, it might appear to be a positive experience. They use it as fuel that challenges them to succeed. For others, it can be just the opposite. It paralyzes them and keeps them from even attempting to succeed. But rest assured, if you're using fear of failure as your primary motivation, eventually it is going to sabotage everything you've worked for.

So, what exactly is failure and how would you define it? How do you know when you've actually failed? Let's use my life as an example. When I went through my divorce, bankruptcy and foreclosure, I definitely felt like a complete failure. It was the most painful and uncomfortable time of my life. It was my thoughts of failure that led to my depression and eventually caused me to consider taking my own life. But had I really failed? According to society, the answer would be *yes*. Our society says that to be successful you must have the house, the wife, the 2.5 kids, the 401K, and you will be successful. Since I had accomplished those things and then lost them, by society's standards I had failed.

This is the trap that too many people fall victim to. We get so attached to titles and labels and "stuff" that we equate them with success. As soon as we lose these things we believe we have failed.

But have we? I believe the answer is no. Although failure may appear to be a negative thing, if we approach it from a spiritual perspective it looks completely different.

Once again, let's use my life as an example.

In retrospect, I can see how my divorce was the absolute best thing that ever happened to me. It was my wake-up call that challenged me to change my life. If not for my divorce I would still be trapped in an unfulfilling marriage, I would still be working in a job I wasn't passionate about, I would have never discovered my gifts of writing and speaking, and therefore I would have never written books that inspire people and help change their lives. In addition, I would have never become a radio show host or a motivational speaker who has inspired countless people around the globe. But most importantly, my divorce challenged me to examine and challenge my most deeply held beliefs about how the Universe works and whether or not there was a Creator of this amazing Universe. My divorce set in motion a series of events that propelled me to discover who I really am and why I am here.

My invitation to you is to be open-minded to the possibility that everything happens for a reason and ultimately the reason is good.

Now, let's tackle the illusion of failure head on so it no longer keeps you from accomplishing your dreams and goals.

First, you must accept there is no such thing as failure. To quote my mentor Dr. Wayne Dyer; "there is no such thing as failure, there is only the non-attainment of a desired result."

In my case, my desired result was a happy family and a comfortable life. During my first marriage, I definitely did not attain my desired result. Did I fail? I don't think so. As mentioned, although I did not attain the result I desired, it eventually led me to that which I truly did desire. When I look at it through spiritual eyes, I can see how the lessons I learned from my first marriage actually taught me how to ensure my second marriage would be better than the first. By being willing to examine the reasons my first marriage didn't work out and then taking 100% responsibility for what I did wrong in that marriage I learned how not to make the same mistakes. So, my first "failed" marriage was simply preparation for me to create the partnership of my dreams, which I currently have.

In regard to the companies, I started and "failed", I can see how each one of them taught me something about business that allowed me to become a better entrepreneur. My "failures" ultimately guided me to find a business I am absolutely passionate about and is a part of my life's purpose. If I had succeeded in any of those other businesses there is a good chance I could have made a lot of money, but my heart wouldn't have been in it and eventually, I'm sure I wouldn't have been successful.

So as an entrepreneur, rest assured there is no need to be afraid of failure because ultimately failure isn't real. It is just a figment of our imagination keeping us from accomplishing our goals.

If you're still struggling with the fear of failure I'd like to share a few ideas to help you deal with it.

According to Vanessa Loder, when we take failure very personally we are always – *always* - associating the failure with a bigger story about ourselves. We are taking the failure to mean "I am not good enough", "I will never be successful as an entrepreneur", "My team is awful", and so on.

When you feel very upset about a specific failure, ask yourself "Hmm, what is the belief I have about this situation?" See if you can uncover the big, hairy exaggerated story you are telling yourself about this particular failure. Try to separate the story from the facts. Facts: A product launch generated $20,000 of revenue compared to the goal of $100,000. Story: My father was right, I'll never make it on my own. I'm a loser.

Once you uncover the story, notice that it is just that. A story. And see if you can re-write it by creating a more positive response such as "I'm willing to take risks, I learn from my mistakes and move on."

The next thing you can do is ask yourself these three powerful questions:

1. What did I learn from this situation?
2. How can I grow as a person from this experience?
3. What are three positive things about this situation?

When you first attempt to list three positive things about the "failure", your mind may be very resistant. But if you stick with the exercise, before you know it, you will see a new opportunity that can come out of this "failure."

For example, you might think; "Well, losing my biggest client gives me time to focus on my smaller clients and sell more to them. And I will also have more time to chase after that other potential new client. And I learned that my product demo needs to be improved, so I can make changes before targeting this new client."

Many of us allow fear to paralyze us because we don't like *feeling* fear. But if you simply allow yourself to feel the fear when it shows up, you will notice it quickly dissipates and suddenly the situation feels more manageable.

The next time you notice yourself getting stressed out or feeling afraid of something not working out, sit quietly by yourself, set your timer for two minutes and start taking deep breaths. Notice where you feel tightness or tension in your body, and simply breathe into that area for the two minutes. When the timer goes off after two minutes, chances are the feelings will have shifted. The more you do this, the more you will trigger your body's natural calm response and you will move through fear with greater ease.

Be sure to take these 3 ideas to heart and do the exercise on a regular basis to help remove your fear of failure if you still have them.

With that being said, let's discuss the big elephant in the room that entrepreneurs seldom talk about - FEAR!

It's been said that fear is the destroyer of dreams and I

couldn't agree more. I'm reminded of a quote from the movie After Earth when Will Smith said:

> "*Fear is not real. The only place that fear can exist is in our thoughts of the future. It is a product of our imagination, causing us to fear things that do not at present and may not ever exist. That is near insanity Kitai. Do not misunderstand me, danger is very real, but fear is a choice. We are all telling ourselves a story and that day mine changed.*"

So, let me make myself abundantly clear. First and foremost, I think it is important for every human being to be able to identify and express their emotions openly and honestly. Feelings are the language of the Soul and they are our internal guidance system, they are neither good nor bad they are just feedback we receive from our own Souls. So, from an emotional perspective, the feeling of fear is very real. But from a spiritual perspective, Will is saying something completely different. He is talking about unwarranted fear created only in our minds that isn't real.

Here are a few examples:

Imagine that you meet someone, and you go on a date. The date goes well, and you decide to start a relationship with them. After a while, you get really close to them, and all of a sudden you become afraid you are going to lose them. You don't know why but all of a sudden you start feeling insecure. You then begin questioning everything they do. Maybe you start checking their phone or reading their emails because you have a fear they might be cheating on you. Your fear is that they will leave you even though they have done absolutely nothing that should cause you to feel the way you do.

Or maybe you're an entrepreneur and you have to make a presentation about your company. Although your company may be doing extremely well you're still a little nervous about making the presentation. The day of the presentation you are overcome with fear. You're afraid that you might screw up the presentation and you begin to have panic attacks as a result of your fear. All of a sudden, you almost become incapacitated based on your fear that you will screw up the presentation.

In both cases, the feeling of fear is very real. But in both cases, the fear is created in the mind, not in reality. There is really no reason to be afraid other than the fact this fear is projecting into a future that hasn't occurred. So, the key to dealing with fear is to stay in the present moment and recognize when you are creating an unwarranted projection of fear that isn't real. It's about taking a deep self-introspective look at what is really driving the fearful thoughts and feelings.

In the case of the relationship, you would have to be willing to examine why you feel so insecure. Maybe it was because someone hurt you in the past or maybe it is because you're terrified of being alone. Ultimately, it boils down to not projecting past pain and fear into the future and that is the reason I mentioned the importance of making peace with your past.

If you're struggling with fear here is a great acronym by Dr. Carmen Harra to remember.

Be FEARLESS

F — Face the truth: Face the truth of your fears. Face what scares you head-on and challenge your trepidation. Separate necessary concerns from baseless fears. Chances are that many of your fears are unwarranted in the greater scheme of your life. Remember, the unfortunate events which you fear will happen do not need to happen.

E — Erase negative imprints: Many times, your fears stem from your own negative experiences or from witnessing the hardships of those around you. Your fear of divorce may very well be rooted in your own parents' divorce. What you must remind yourself daily — through simple affirmations or guided visualizations — is that your past is your past, and whatever happened in your past, which makes you afraid today, must be dealt with and its mental imprints removed permanently.

A — Allow change: People are by nature afraid of change. They fear that change will somehow disrupt their lives or uproot them from their comfort zone. But change actually serves to transport us into new, greater manifestations of ourselves. Allow necessary changes to come your way, even if they may seem frightening at first. Every instance of change serves a purpose towards your highest good, and you will learn this in time.

R — Relax: Fear can be the accumulation of too much stress or extended pressure. A hectic life with too many responsibilities results in fear of failure. It's essential you take time out for yourself to relax and meditate and alleviate your anxieties. So, calm down, take a breather, and remind yourself you will be shown how to resolve all things.

L — Listen to your intuition: If you learn how to follow it, your intuition can banish your fears. This is because your intuition is like a mental GPS into the future, so you can sense what's to come and where you need to go and ease your apprehensions of what tomorrow might hold.

E — End feuds: When you fight with others, you draw fear into your relationships: fear that others will betray, hurt, or abandon you. In order to nurture fearlessness, you must make peace with those around you and understand that their intentions are not to cause you harm.

S — Selectivity: You have to learn to be selective about what you want out of life and the things you decide to go after. You have to pursue things which don't inspire fear in you and make you feel completely comfortable. Select a vision for your future and stick to that mental projection until you've brought it fully to life.

S - Secure in yourself: In order to shun fear forever, you have to work on your self-esteem. Fear arises from not believing enough in your own abilities and talents. When you constantly live in the mindset of "I can't do it" or, "I'm not good enough," you narrow your window of success to a very slim opening and inadvertently put yourself down.

Although the role of fear is to keep us safe, we do ourselves no favor by living in it. To awaken our potential and draw in bigger possibilities, we must eradicate fear from our lives through daily efforts which promote our strength and self-security. After all, we all possess the inherent trait of everlasting courage which can guide us through most anything.

~ ~ ~

There should be no shame in admitting you feel fear. Fear is a natural part of being human. Your challenge is to constantly face your fears and overcome them. When you learn to overcome your fears and not let them keep you from accomplishing your goals you lay the foundation for creating an extraordinary life and living the life you were born to live.

So, remember: there is no such thing as failure, there is only the non-attainment of a desired result. Commit to becoming FEARLESS and you will become unstoppable.

"Everyone has his own specific vocation or mission in life; everyone must carry out a concrete assignment that demands fulfillment. Therein he cannot be replaced, nor can his life be repeated; thus, everyone's task is unique as his specific opportunity to implement it."

Viktor E. Frankl

Chapter 9

Moonshots & MTPs

On May 25, 1961, President John F. Kennedy stood before Congress and announced his goal of putting a man on the moon by the end of the decade.

His decision was driven by the fact that the Russians had beat the Americans into space and he believed America could regain its position as a world leader in space exploration if they were able to land on the moon first.

Here is an excerpt from that speech:

"First, I believe that this nation should commit itself to achieving the goal, before this decade is out, of landing a man on the moon and returning him safely to the Earth. No single space project in this period will be more impressive to mankind, or more important for the long-range exploration of space, and none will be so difficult or expensive to accomplish. We propose to accelerate the development of the appropriate lunar spacecraft. We propose to develop alternate liquid and solid fuel boosters, much larger than any now being developed, until certain, which is superior. We propose additional funds for other engine development and for unmanned exploration - explorations which are particularly important for one purpose which this nation will never overlook: the survival of the man who first makes this daring flight. But in a very real sense, it will not be one man going to the moon - if we make this judgment affirmatively, it will be an entire nation. For all of us must work to put him there."

Approximately two-and-a-half years after giving the speech, Kennedy was assassinated. Just over eight years after the speech, on July 20, 1969, NASA's Apollo 11 mission would land the first humans on the moon.

To this day I believe this is one of the most inspiring accomplishments the world has ever seen. What inspires me the most is President Kennedy's vision and commitment to do something that had never been done before. Although most people believed it was impossible at the time, he intuitively knew it was possible, and he made a commitment to make it happen.

President Kennedy set a Moonshot goal and he committed to bringing it to reality. And although he didn't live to see it happen, his vision and commitment to land a man on the moon was brought to fruition by a nation that believed in him and would not let his vision die. His vision was big enough and bold enough that the entire nation embraced it and the American people supported it and brought it to reality.

As an entrepreneur, it's important to have "Moonshot" goals. Goals that may seem impossible or audacious to others, but to you, they are achievable. One of my favorite quotes is: "Do not let reality stand in the way of your dreams. Only you determine what's realistic or not."

So, take a moment and try to imagine how President Kennedy felt and how he thought about his dream of placing a man on the moon. In his mind, he knew it could be done even when the "experts" probably told him it wasn't possible. In his heart of hearts, he knew it was possible. How did he know that? How and why was he able to "see" this vision and then be able to manifest it?

Once again, I refer to the Infinite Intelligence that created the Universe. President Kennedy was tuned in to the Universal Radio and he received a signal, which is really a divine idea from Infinite Intelligence. Ideas are the currency of the Universe and when we are tuned in to our specific channel we receive unique individual ideas that are specifically sent to us. Once the idea was planted in his mind he then had to take action to bring the idea to life. I'm sure he consulted with engineers and experts from NASA to confirm the viability of such a mission, and once confirmed he decided to share his vision with the world and gained the courage to propose to Congress that it was a goal he wanted to reach. By enrolling Congress into his dream, he then gained the support of an entire nation to bring his dream to reality.

This story is the perfect metaphor for being an entrepreneur. Every business idea is literally a Moonshot idea. In order to build your business, you must be willing to set S.M.A.R.T. goals and accomplish them. I'd like to break down what S. M. A. R. T. goals are and how you can use them to launch your very own Moonshot goal.

SMART

Specific
Measurable
Attainable
Relevant
Time-Bound

Specific

Everything that has ever been created on this planet began as a simple idea in someone's mind. The clothes you're wearing, the chair you're sitting in, the book you're reading, the television you watch, and the car you drive all began as single thoughts in the mind of a single human being.

If you accept my theory that Infinite Intelligence is the source of divine ideas, then you should recognize that your Moonshot idea comes directly from Infinite Intelligence. It is a unique "signal" sent from the Universal Radio. As an entrepreneur, you must receive this signal and then focus all your attention on it. This is what it means by having a vision - you've received the signal and now you are open to the idea that you can actually manifest the vision into your life.

Once received, it's important you write it down and not just think about it. Ideas are fleeting and can disappear in an instant. To solidify the idea in your mind it's imperative that you put it down on paper. Once you've written it down it then becomes a goal. Unfortunately, very few people are willing to do this and that is the primary reason most people do not accomplish their goals. They never write them down. Writing them down makes them specific. It also sends a signal back to the Universal Radio that you're listening and have received the idea. When you do this, you will begin to receive more signals from the radio.

Measurable

Once your idea becomes specific you must then set up measurable milestones that let you know you're moving in the direction of your dreams. As an entrepreneur, a great place to start is by putting together a business plan outlining everything you need to launch your business. A business plan allows you to have a birds-eye-view of your business and it should guide you along your unique path to success. The key is to know where you're going and how you plan on getting there. Setting measurable goals guides you along your journey. For example, your first goal could be to put together a business plan. A measurable goal would be the completion of the plan. Once the goal of putting the business plan is set then you will set measurable goals for completion. There are basically 7 essential sections of a business plan, these are:

1. Executive Summary
2. Company Description
3. Products and Services
4. Market Analysis
5. Strategy and Implementation
6. Organization and Management Team

7. Financial Plan and Projections.

Set measurable goals to put these 7 sections together until your business plan is complete.

Achievable

This one will be between you and Infinite Intelligence. Only you can determine what's achievable for you. I believe it's important to set unrealistic goals and then create realistic steps to create them. Most people will tell you to be realistic, but I say only *you* can determine what realistic is. Was it realistic for the Wright Brothers to decide to create the first airplane? Absolutely not! Most people thought they were insane, but we all know how that turned out.

This is another reason why having a connection to Infinite Intelligence is so important.

Remember the earlier quote I shared by Deepak Chopra? "Inherent in every intention and desire are the mechanics for its fulfillment." When Infinite Intelligence sends you the signal you must be willing to trust in your ability to manifest it. You already have everything you need to manifest the idea inside you, otherwise, you would have not received the signal.

Relevant

Relevance can be defined as; *practical* and especially *social applicability*. In other words, how relevant are your products or services in today's marketplace? The adage of "find a need and fill it" applies here. If you can identify a specific need and create a solution to that need then you have relevance.

Time-Bound

When President Kennedy declared he wanted to land a man on the moon he set a goal of accomplishing it within a decade. He didn't give a specific date, but he did commit to attaining it in a certain timeframe. This is important to remember. Having a quantifiable timeline for your goals is extremely important but not something you have to be extremely rigid about. In other words, be sure to put specific timeframes on accomplishing your goals but be flexible and realize that sometimes you will not hit those targets. From a spiritual perspective, the Universe's delays are not necessarily denials. Sometimes things will just take longer than you anticipate so don't beat yourself up for not hitting your target dates. Of course, there will be times when you have to meet certain deadlines and you do not want to miss them, but in general, when setting goals write them down, set a date for completion, and work your tail off until you accomplish them.

~ ~ ~

So, what's your Moonshot? What is that dream you've been thinking about but haven't taken any action on yet? Here is a great opportunity for you to get started. Right now, I simply want you to write down that idea you've had but haven't put it to paper yet. Complete this sentence:

My Moonshot idea is_____

You must remember that Infinite Intelligence responds to your responses. When you receive a signal and then write it down it tells Infinite Intelligence you're serious and you're ready and willing to manifest that idea. Writing it down is the very first step.

Did you take it?

~ ~ ~

Once you've grasped the concept of Moonshots it's time for you to grasp something much deeper and impactful as an entrepreneur. I've talked a lot about the Universal Radio and the signals that it sends to us. I've shared how ideas are the currency of the Universe and I've shared the importance of developing a relationship with yourself as the cornerstone of success. And now I want to share arguably the most important idea in this book.

The most important message I must share with you is that **you have a Divine Purpose**. Whether you believe it or not, I can assure you it's true. There is something you were specifically put on this planet to do, and it is your responsibility to figure out what it is. As a matter of fact, I believe your purpose is encoded within your DNA and it is as unique and individuated as your fingerprints. The Universe never duplicates itself. There is only one you and you are one of a kind.

In this context, there are two types of purpose. There is your entrepreneurial purpose and your spiritual purpose.

As an entrepreneur, your purpose is to discover your

MTP, Massively Transformative Purpose. If you aren't interested in the spiritual woo-woo stuff, finding your MTP can still be very rewarding and fulfilling and it can lead you to creating a very successful enterprise.

If you want to go deeper and are open to the spiritual woo-woo stuff, finding your Divine Purpose is definitely the goal you want to pursue. As a human being, your Divine Purpose is to awaken to your authentic self and your divine expression as a human being.

Finding your MTP should be your top priority as an entrepreneur. Most entrepreneurs have heard of vision and mission statements but very few of them have ever heard of an MTP. According to Alison E. Berman, an MTP could be described as a highly aspirational tagline for an individual or group, like a company, organization, community, or social movement.

She defines Massive as:

> *"Audacious big and aspirational",* Transformative as *"Can cause significant transformation to an industry, community, or to the planet"* and Purpose as *"There's a clear "why" behind the work being done. Something that unites and inspires action."*

For me, my MTP for my company is: *to empower individuals to transform themselves from the inside out and awaken them to who they really are so they can transform the world.*

So, what is your MTP? Don't worry if you have never heard of or created an MTP before. This is the reason you're reading this book - to gain insights and wisdom to help you become a better entrepreneur.

If you would like to create your own MTP here are two things Peter Diamandis says you need to focus on to identify your purpose.

1. Identify the Who: Ask yourself who you want to impact. What community do you want to create a lasting positive impact on? Is it high school students? The elderly? People suffering a chronic disease? These are just a few examples of potential groups to focus your purpose towards.

2. Identify the What: What problem do you want to take on and solve? Here's an exercise created by Diamandis to identify the "what" of your purpose:

Step one: Write down the **top three items** you are most excited about or get you most riled up (that you want to solve).

Step two: For each of the three problems listed above, ask the following six questions and score each from 1-10 (1 = small difference, 10 = big difference)

ASSESSMENT QUESTIONS

1. If, at the end of your life, you had made a significant dent in this area, how proud would you feel?
2. Given the resources you have today, what level of impact could you make in the next three years if you solved this problem?

3. Given the resources you expect to have in 10 years, what level of impact could you make in a 3-year period?

4. How well do you understand the problem?

5. How emotionally charged (excited or riled up) are you about this?

6. Will this problem get solved with or without you involved?

TOTAL = Add up your scores and identify the idea with the highest score. This is your winner for now. Does this one intuitively feel right to you?

Take some time to do the exercise and see if you can come up with your MTP. You may have to do it several times to find it but if you commit to it eventually you will discover it.

For those of you who are open-minded and want to go a lot deeper, I highly recommend you commit to finding your Divine Purpose. When you do, your MTP will show up automatically.

Finding your Divine Purpose falls under the spiritual category. Remember, you do not have to be religious to be spiritual. You do not have to practice or adhere to any religious dogma or doctrine and you do not have to be attached to any labels. Your spirituality is between you and Infinite Intelligence and how you express that and connect to it is entirely up to you.

Finding your Divine Purpose is a process. I do not have any special training or credentials in doing this, so I simply want to share some things I've learned over the past couple of decades that has allowed me to discover my purpose and create my version of an extraordinary life.

First, I believe you *do* have a Divine Purpose and there is a part of you that already knows what it is. To explain this, I would like to share an excerpt from the book: *True Purpose* by Tim Kelley and I highly recommend you pick up a copy of his book because it is filled with wisdom that will guide you to your Divine Purpose.

"I contended at the very beginning that you already have a purpose and that part of you already knows what it is. I am going to call that part of you your "soul." This is a loaded term, and different religious and spiritual traditions define it in many different ways. I do not intend to invoke religious definitions; for the purposes of this book I am simply defining "soul" to mean "the part of you that knows your purpose." I use this word because, of the thousands of words that most people use on a regular basis, it comes closest to what I mean. Of course, you are free to add whatever personal meaning you want to the term. Later, we will expand this term and encourage you to replace the word "soul" with language that is more specific and meaningful for you.

If you don't already know your purpose, then your purpose and your soul are both in your unconscious. Remember, the unconscious is by definition those things you don't know about yourself. There are many other things in your unconscious, but the part that interests us in this exploration is your soul because it is the keeper of your purpose.

This is one of the points in the process where your religious and spiritual beliefs come into play. For example, if you are a monotheist (a Christian, Jew, Muslim, or Bahá'í, to name a few) then I would say that your soul is your interface to God. God put your soul in you to guide you and to remember your purpose so that it wouldn't be lost when you forgot. If you are an agnostic or atheist, or if your beliefs do not include a singular God, then what I just wrote is irrelevant for you. Your soul is simply part of your design. It is the part responsible for knowing your purpose, in the same way your kidneys are responsible for filtering your blood and your ears are responsible for hearing. A belief in God is not required for most of the methods in this book to work. The soul's responsibilities are very different from the ego's. The soul is not concerned with preserving your identity or your day-to-day safety and needs. It is charged with entirely different things.

The soul is the keeper of your purpose. It knows everything about who you are, including the things you have disowned and forgotten. It knows who you are meant to be and what you are meant to do. It makes decisions about how much of your purpose you are ready to know. I'll discuss this further later.

The soul is charged with your growth and development. Your soul isn't that concerned about how much money you are making at work and whether or not you like your job. It cares whether you are learning, growing, and transforming from the experience. Your soul may sometimes guide you towards unpleasant things so that you will develop or learn in specific ways. This is very confusing for the ego, which is usually trying to avoid pain and failure as best it can. Your soul is not trying to create just any growth and learning; it is trying to develop you in very specific ways that will serve your purpose. Your soul is going through its checklist of skills and experiences that you will need in order to fulfill your purpose. Its job is to make sure that the checklist is complete, that you have everything you need."

Another way to look at Soul is as your unique station on the Universal Radio. It has direct access to Infinite Intelligence and is unique to you as a human being. If you are going to find your Divine Purpose, then it's important that you accept this idea. Finding your purpose is like tuning in to your particular station. At times your connection may be filled with static, but as you fine-tune and focus eventually you will land directly on your station and the signal will come in loud and clear.

To tune in to your Divine Purpose it's also important for you to understand the Four Stages of Purpose as proposed by Brandon Peele in his phenomenal book *Planet on Purpose* (you should also pick up a copy of it immediately if you're interested in finding your divine purpose).

In the book, he shares four stages that will guide you in finding your unique purpose and I would like to share them with you now.

Stage 1: No Purpose

This stage is where you have no known purpose or are ignoring the calls to live purposefully. You might content yourself with life's simple pleasures and just sort of float from one experience to another, chasing pleasure, avoiding pain, and dealing with life's circumstances as they arise, regarding them as beyond your control. It's perfectly fine to be in this stage. Many people are content to live their entire lives without an explicit relationship to their life's purpose or the power to create a bigger life of impact, abundance, connection, and fulfillment. More often than not, however, this stage is temporary. I learned the hard way that living without purpose creates problems, like a pattern of unfulfilling relationships and jobs, depression, ER visits, addiction, arrests, and other health concerns. However, this is a vital stage, as it presents the largest opportunity for growth. This is the fertile soil from which the desire for a life's purpose grows.

Stage 2: Declared Purpose

This stage is where you simply declare you have a purpose, really any purpose. You say you want to be skinny, or be a Marine, or be wealthy, or build an app, or be number one in your industry, or even declare that you want to find your higher purpose, your soul's purpose. It's perfectly fine to have a declared purpose but know this is a purpose that comes from your ego and is rooted in the concerns, social values, and cultural mores of your upbringing. It is not rooted in the deeper identity of your soul.

Stage 3: Higher Purpose

This stage is available to you after doing purpose discovery work, wherein all ten aspects of your soul's purpose are revealed to you as true and sourced internally. Access to your higher purpose also includes a process wherein you get to understand the source of your resistance to living your purpose, the disempowering narratives and limiting beliefs that keep you from taking purpose-aligned action. So, in addition to having the clarity, confidence, and certainty of your higher purpose, you also have the power to be unstoppable in living and leading with your purpose. By unstoppable, I mean you won't hear "no" as a reason to stop. You won't get stopped by your reasons/internal resistance. "No" will simply mean, "try it another way." A bad mood will simply mean that it is time to create a new enlivening context and act. Your higher purpose grants you the grit and tools required to overcome the obstacles in your way.

Stage 4: Unitive Purpose

This is the stage wherein your higher purpose descends and integrates into your tissues as a way of being, and also goes global in the form of leadership. In this stage, you begin to function as, of, by, and for the whole Cosmos and experience Unitive Purpose. To move into and through the Unitive Stage you have three key tasks:

1. Mentorship - where you seek out mentorship, books, and programs from masters germane to your craft and mission.

2. Integrate and Embody - a multiple-year process of aligning and upgrading every key area of your life to express your purpose, such that you move effortlessly and seamlessly between contexts and circumstances fully rooted, embodied, and integrated.

3. Purpose-aligned Action - with your mentors and masters at your side, and an explicit relationship to your expanding worldview, you now are called to act, express, and lead with your purpose.

Mentorship

As every soul, craft, and vision is unique, every soul's need for mentors is unique. In the discovery process, your soul will reveal to you your masters and mentors. You will read their books, take their programs, and when you feel the call, you will work directly with one or more of them. For example, when I became clear that purpose guiding was essential to my craft, I identified the leading voices in the field (Bill Plotkin, Jonathan Gustin, Tim Kelley, Rod Stryker, Michael Meade), read their books and began my training and certification with Jonathan Gustin at the Purpose Guides Institute.

Integrate and Embody

Your access to embodying your purpose and your ever-expanding worldview is through your integrity - becoming a leader who is the walking embodiment of purpose, taking consistent action, learning and reconciling all areas of your life (health, career, romance, family, community, finances, spirituality) with your purpose. Once you are through the purpose discovery process, you'll see the necessary alignment changes you need to make in these key life areas such that your day-to-day life is the perfect container and support system for your soul's purpose. You'll likely take on leadership programs, as well as spiritual, contemplative, somatic and integrative practices such as yoga, cross-training, and martial arts to descend this new soul identity into your tissues. As you move through Part Two, you will explore integrity and leadership as the keys to the integration/unitive phase of your purpose journey.

Purpose-aligned Action

The discovery process is only the beginning of your purpose journey. Your access to staying connected to your soul is active - crafting and completing missions/your Purpose Projects. In the active expressions of your purpose, you will learn more by a factor of ten about your soul's purpose than in the initial discovery phase. You will see how your purpose must rise to meet the world as it is, how it needs to evolve and expand to make an even greater impact, and how you will need to grow, develop, and expand to contain and support the expansion of your purposeful impact in the world. As you move through Parts Three and Four of this book you will discover these new horizons of impact.

Now you understand the evolution and progression of your relationship to purpose, you need only declare what kind of purpose you want. Simply state that you wish to have no purpose (Stage 1) and just experience life as it comes. That's perfectly fine. Or you can declare a purpose right now (Stage 2). Just pick a person you admire, or an outcome deemed desirable by others, declare yourself to be that person's disciple or in service of that desired outcome. That's also perfectly fine. Or you can reveal your higher purpose (Stage 3), by doing the work in Part Two and moving through the world with a deep understanding of who you are and what you came to do. This is also perfectly fine. Or you can declare that you will lead humanity in fulfilling its purpose (Stage 4), by unleashing your purpose, embodying it, meaningfully evolving your worldview beginning with Part Three, by choosing your masters and mentors, and playing a big game that elevates the whole human and ecological condition, beginning in Part Four. Before you go any further, I request you take a moment to reflect: Which type of purpose feels most aligned with who you really are inside?

As mentioned, you get to decide which stage of purpose you are going to be in. There is no right or wrong, good or bad when it comes to choosing. It's really a matter of how you feel and how connected you are to Infinite Intelligence. So, choose wisely.

~ ~ ~

As I reflect over the last 25 years of my life I can see how I actually went through these four stages. One of the reasons I became a writer and a speaker is because they are both divine gifts bestowed on me by Infinite Intelligence and I feel a deep responsibility to share my gifts with the world to make it a better place. This is what occurs when you move into Stage 4 Unitive Purpose. You become aware of your oneness with all of life and you feel a pull and a responsibility to help heal the planet and support others in waking up to their own divinity.

There are no shortcuts to finding your Divine Purpose, but I hope this chapter has challenged you to at least think about your purpose. You may not know this but there are no accidents in a perfect Universe. Therefore, there is a

Divine Reason you are reading this book right now and it is quite possible that your goal in reading this book is to guide you to discover your purpose.

But remember, finding your purpose is a choice and your mission if you choose it, is to find your purpose and your gifts and share them with the world.

Mission, Possible!

"Never doubt that a small group of thoughtful, committed citizens can change the world; indeed, it's the only thing that ever has."

Margaret Mead

Chapter 10

Side Hustles and Solopreneurs

According to a 2017 Gallup Poll, 85% of the people surveyed said they hated their job. It didn't say they did not like their job, it said they *hated* their job. So, take a moment and ask yourself, if someone hates their job, how effective and productive will that person be?

It doesn't take a rocket scientist to figure out the answer. If you hate something, there is no way you could actually do your best at it.

Another interesting statistic I ran across in The Guardian said that 80% of US workers live from paycheck to paycheck. Which is staggering to me considering that we live in the wealthiest country in the world. In a country filled with such wealth, how in the world do we end up with these two statistics?

To answer the question of why 80% of people hate their jobs, I want to share "The Top Four Reasons People Hate Their Jobs" by Maurie Backman. Her article was based on data shared by the website hired.com.

1. Few or little opportunity for advancement

There's nothing worse than the feeling of knowing you're stuck in a dead-end job. It's no wonder, then, that having virtually no chance of getting ahead is the thing that bums working Americans out the most.

If you're stuck in a job with no real future, the solution is simple: put yourself out there and find a better opportunity. You may need to do some serious networking to get there, whether it's aggressively reaching out to industry contacts or attending conferences in the hopes of snagging an opening somewhere. You may even have to work on building up some of your skills to ensure you're qualified for a more desirable role, which could mean taking a class or renewing a certification. But no matter what specific steps end up being involved, the key is to get out of a dead-end situation before your performance and sanity start to suffer.

2. Company culture

It's one thing for your employer to expect that you show up on time and work your hardest during business hours, but it's another thing to work in an environment where 50 hours a week on the job is nowhere near respectable and leaving at 5:00 p.m. is considered a half-day. In fact, another major reason why so many folks can't stand their jobs is that they're just plain unhappy with the company culture they're subjected to.

If you feel your company's culture is rooted in unreasonable demands, and that employees just aren't respected across the board, it's time to work somewhere that better aligns with your personality and expectations. Finding the ideal fit isn't easy, but once you identify some leads, do your research to see how employees tend to be treated. This might mean reaching out to people you know at those companies or checking out anonymous company reviews on sites like Glassdoor.

3. Being underpaid

Not shockingly, a large chunk of working Americans is dissatisfied with their paychecks. If you're convinced you're being underpaid, you have one of two choices: find a better-paying job elsewhere or gear up to negotiate a raise.

The latter might actually be less intimidating than you'd think, provided you come prepared. To successfully fight for a raise, do your research to see what other professionals in your industry are making. Sites like Salary.com make it easy to see how your compensation stacks up based on your job title and geographic location.

Once you've compiled some data, make a list of your accomplishments to date, and show the powers that be at your company why you're such a valuable asset. If you can simultaneously prove that you're not getting the going rate and that your employer truly needs you, there's a good chance you'll score that much-needed salary bump.

4. Loathsome managers and coworkers

Sometimes, the people you work with, and for, can make or break your experience on the job. Given the amount of time some of us spend at the office, it's not surprising to learn that a large number of Americans are unhappy at work primarily because of the people they're surrounded by. But while dealing with a toxic co-worker or terrible boss is no picnic, there are ways to mitigate your suffering if you're otherwise happy where you are.

If it's an annoying or unscrupulous colleague who's bringing you down, your best bet is to distance yourself from that person to the greatest extent possible. Ask to be assigned to a different project or team and do your best to carve out a position that keeps your interactions with that dreaded coworker to a minimum. If that's not an option, document any and all incidents in which that person steps over the line. If you have a decent human resources department, someone will have no choice but to intervene.

Dealing with an awful boss is far more challenging, but if you do your best to understand what sets your manager off, you can take steps to avoid those scenarios, thus minimizing conflict. You might also try talking things out with your boss, assuming they are a minimally reasonable human being. If that doesn't work, there's always the option to ask for a transfer to another department or team. And don't hesitate to keep a log of interactions where your boss acts inappropriately so that you have a leg to stand on if an HR conversation becomes necessary.

~ ~ ~

So now I must ask you a couple of questions. 1. Are you happy with your current job? 2. Are you living paycheck to paycheck?

It's been said that the first step to solving any problem is to admit there is one. Be completely honest with yourself and admit if there is a problem.

If the answer is yes, are you interested in a possible solution?

I am 100% convinced that the solution to your problem is to become an entrepreneur. Remember my definition of entrepreneur? It is someone who receives compensation in exchange for a product or service. Becoming an entrepreneur does not necessarily mean you will be building a company. It means you are open to having a Side Hustle or becoming a Solopreneur.

The first thing an entrepreneur must do is take 100% responsibility for their lives turning out the way they want it to. This means you will no longer point fingers and place blame on anyone except yourself. You can no longer blame your terrible boss, the government, your race, or your ex-husband/wife. You cannot blame your age or your educational level or the family you grew up in. If you're in a situation that you dislike the only one who can change it is *you*. You must embrace the motto: "If it's to be, it's up to me!"

Once you've taken responsibility for your life, the next step is to see what options you have to change your situation. If you're stuck in a job with no real future, the solution is simple: Put yourself out there and find a better opportunity. The first obvious solution you have is to simply find another job. This can definitely be difficult and challenging but rest assured it's doable. Let me repeat what Maurie Backman said in her article:

If you're stuck in a job with no real future, the solution is simple: Put yourself out there and find a better opportunity. You may need to do some serious networking to get there, whether it's aggressively reaching out to industry contacts or attending conferences in the hopes of snagging an opening somewhere. You may even have to work on building up some of your skills to ensure that you're qualified for a more desirable role, which could mean taking a class or renewing a certification. But no matter what specific steps end up being involved, the key is to get out of a dead-end situation before your performance and sanity start to suffer.

If you like your job but hate your boss what options do you have that could change the situation? Can you speak with someone in HR to see about resolving whatever issue you have with your boss? Can you get transferred to another department or location? Can you have a heart-to-heart conversation with your boss that might change their attitude?

None of these things is easy, but you must begin somewhere. You must be willing to take some actions to change your situation and it all begins with you.

Another solution to consider if you're living paycheck to paycheck is to find a Side Hustle. A Side Hustle is another way of becoming an entrepreneur. The good news is there are unlimited opportunities out there if you're willing to find them. A Side Hustle is a way of bringing in additional money, but it can also lead to starting a new career or vocation.

Here is a list of 10 Side Hustles you might consider.

1. Uber

- Make money by driving people around town
- Set your own hours and availability
- If you don't have your own car, you can rent through Uber
- Must pass a background check and have a clean driving record

2. Turo

- Rent out your car as a passive income source
- Make up to $600 per month
- Set your own rates and your car's availability
- Turo provides comprehensive insurance coverage

3. Amazon Flex

- Deliver packages for Amazon for extra money
- Pays $18 to $25 an hour
- Set your own schedule and work whenever you want
- You must have a smartphone and your own vehicle
- Must pass a background check

4. Postmates

- Deliver food, office supplies, and more to customers in your area

- Earn up to $25 an hour
- Set your own availability (only required to make one delivery every 90 days)
- You must have a smartphone and your own vehicle

5. DoorDash

- Earn money by delivering restaurant food to customers
- Earn over $10 an hour
- Set your own schedule, including working early mornings or late nights
- You need an Android or iOS smartphone
- Must pass a background check

6. Shipt

- Shop and deliver groceries for customers
- You can make an average of $15 to $25 an hour
- Work whenever is convenient for you and take a vacation when you want
- Must have reliable transportation
- Must pass a background check

7. VRBO

- Rent a spare bed or your whole house
- Top owners who use VRBO to rent out their properties make up to $60,000 per year
- Set your own rates and room availability
- Rent whenever it is convenient for you

8. Handy

- Great side gig for professional cleaners and handymen
- Earn up to $22 and $45 an hour, depending on the task
- Payments are directly deposited after each job
- Determine your own availability and work schedule

9. Dolly

- If you're capable of moving large items like furniture, you can make up to $15 an hour as a mover
- If you have a truck or cargo van, you can make even more money (workers who provide a vehicle and labor can make up to $30 an hour)
- Must be able to lift at least 75 pounds
- Using the app, you can accept gigs that fit your schedule

10. Zeel

- Must be a licensed massage therapist
- Perform in-home massages and keep 75 percent of the booking fee
- Zeel automatically adds 18 percent gratuity to the bill, which you keep
- Accept jobs when it's convenient for you

If you're looking to increase your monthly income immediately be sure to check out these Side Hustles. The key here is to understand that you have options to change your life so be sure to take advantage of these possible opportunities.

If you're ready to completely change your life and be your own boss, then it's time for you to consider becoming a Solopreneur. A Solopreneur is also an entrepreneur that is a single individual who builds and runs their own company without any other employees.

The good news is it's never been easier to become a Solopreneur. Anyone with a skill or a passion can become a Solopreneur. Maybe you enjoy writing, so you decide to launch a blog. Or maybe you love teaching, so you launch a YouTube channel. Do you love to have deep stimulating conversations and talking to people? Then maybe you could become a podcaster and launch an online podcast. There are infinite opportunities out there for anyone who has a passion for something and is willing to share their passion with others.

Did you know that Solopreneurs are making millions of dollars a year doing what they love? Case in point, there is a six-year-old boy named Ryan who has a YouTube channel called 'Ryan's Toy Review'. Currently, he has more than 16 million subscribers to his channel and makes millions of dollars a year reviewing toys. Ryan is a perfect example of how to turn your passion into profits by doing what you love.

I'm sure there are some of you reading this who may be saying *I can't become a solopreneur because I already have a job and I have to provide for my family.* To which I reply, at the time of this writing, I am currently employed at a hardware store as a floor supervisor and electrical department manager. I work approximately 50 hours a week on a 5-day schedule. I actually enjoy my job and have been working there for 18 years.

Although I work a fulltime job, I am also a Solopreneur who is building a publishing company. Writing books and being a motivational speaker are my passions but at this point, I do not generate enough revenue to quit my day job. My goal, however, is to build my publishing company and eventually be able to leave my regular 9-to-5 job. Although I would much rather be working full time on my own company, until my business revenue exceeds my current salary I will stay put.

This is what it takes to be an entrepreneur. You must sometimes be willing to make sacrifices while you are building your company. For those of you who may be saying you don't have enough time let me suggest that there is no such thing as not enough time, there is only a lack of desire. If the desire is strong enough rest assured, you will *make* the time.

As a Solopreneur I have to do it all. I am the bookkeeper, the marketer, the website designer, the writer, the videographer, the video editor, the audio engineer, the blogger, and the leader. I am responsible for everything. If something goes wrong guess who is responsible for figuring out how to fix it? I am!

For some people, this would be overwhelming. It seems like just too much to do. Working full time while building a business isn't easy or for the faint of heart or weak-minded.

It takes intelligence, patience, persistence, perseverance, creativity, tons of faith, and an incredible amount of discipline. But this is the path I have chosen to take and since you're reading this right now I am going to assume it is a path you are considering and possibly willing to take also.

I'd like to share some lessons and some benefits of being a Solopreneur in the hopes it inspires you and challenges you to join the ranks of the self-employed if that is your goal.

Since spiritual compensation is my top compensation priority, I have to begin by saying that I am driven by something deep inside me that I can't explain in words. The best way to describe it would be to say I have a deep burning desire to create and express the Infinite Intelligence that is within me. It is this Divine Energy within me that drives me and gives me the vision, the courage, and the strength to move through any obstacle and stay focused on my goals. As I mentioned earlier, I've known since I was approximately 10 years old exactly what I wanted to be when I grew up and I firmly believe it is because I began receiving the Universal Radio's signal at that time.

I'm reminded of the story of Nelson Mandela who spent 27 years in prison and yet held on to his dream to one day become president of South Africa and end Apartheid. I have always been fascinated and inspired by his story and have always used it whenever I felt down or unsure of whether or not I could live my dreams. As I think about his life story I refer to the analogy of the Universal Radio. As I've mentioned throughout this book, Infinite Intelligence is the Source of divine ideas. By tuning in to his divine channel on the Universal Radio I believe Nelson Mandela awakened to his divine purpose and by trusting Infinite Intelligence, he was able to find the faith and the strength to ultimately fill his divine destiny.

Once again, I believe that every human being has access to this Infinite Intelligence. If you're reading this right now you too have access to this Intelligence. It's just a matter of tuning in to your unique channel and learning how to hear and trust whenever you receive divine signals from the Universe.

For me, everything begins and ends with my connection to Infinite Intelligence. And I highly suggest you develop your own connection to the Universal Radio, so you can receive your unique signals that will guide you to your ultimate destiny. I believe this is the first step to being a happy entrepreneur.

Next, you must be willing to declare what you want. In other words, you must have a vision of what you want to create. Do you want to be a Solopreneur or do you want to build a business with multiple employees? Or maybe you're dreaming a little bigger and want to build a billion-dollar corporation with hundreds of employees that cover the globe. No matter what your goal is, you must be willing to put that vision down on paper in some way, so the Universe can begin to work with you to create your vision.

Next, you must be willing to learn new things and take

advantage of current technology. Remember, as a human being you have an infinite capacity for learning and therefore you must be willing to learn new things in order to succeed. Alvin Toffler once said: "the functional illiterate of the 21st century will not be those who cannot read or write, both those who cannot learn, unlearn, and relearn." You must be willing to learn, unlearn, and relearn on a constant basis if you want to be a successful entrepreneur.

The real advantage of being willing to learn, unlearn, and relearn as an entrepreneur is the amount of money you can save yourself and your company by learning to do things yourself. One advantage I have is I love technology. I love everything about evolving technology. I love computers, the Internet, electronic gadgets, cell phones - you name it I love it if it has something to do with tech. Of course, when you truly love something it doesn't feel like work to learn it. It feels more like play, so I'm constantly playing with tech while learning at the same time.

I recently put together some estimates of how much money I saved over a one-year period by doing things myself. A very conservative estimate was well over 20 thousand dollars. This includes building my own websites (6 at the time of this writing), building an app, hosting Webinars, hosting 2 podcasts and launching an E-Commerce store. All these things I learned how to do from the comfort of my home office with little to no cost at all.

What really made this easy was the Internet. It truly amazes me how much you can learn on YouTube and other free online resources. Whenever I need to learn something the first thing I normally do is log on to YouTube and see if there are any videos on the subject I want to learn. In most cases, I can find an instructional video that teaches me whatever it is I'm trying to learn at no cost whatsoever. Learning is FREE!

The only thing that can keep you from becoming an entrepreneur is *you*. If you have a burning desire within you to be your own boss and control your own destiny the doors of opportunity are wide open, all you have to do is walk through them.

I want to circle back to the comment, "When you do what you love the money will follow." As mentioned, this holds true only if you're willing to learn how to market and promote yourself and your business. But my point here is the importance of doing what you love. It is imperative for you to discover the things you love and the things you are good at. You definitely have some unique gifts and talents within you that you must be willing to let out. By locating these things you love, you will then tap into Infinite Intelligence and then you can convert those things into a thriving business.

In summary, connect to Infinite Intelligence, find your gifts, share your gifts, and build your business. It's all up to you.

"To excel at the highest level - or any level, really - you need to believe in yourself, and hands down, one of the biggest contributors to my self-confidence has been private coaching."

Stephen Curry

Chapter 11
The Power of Coaching

What do Serena Williams, Tom Brady, Lebron James, Justin Verlander and Tiger Woods all have in common? Your immediate answer is probably that they are all incredible athletes. You may also say they are all very rich celebrities. Of course, each of these answers would be correct, but there is one thing that connects them and they all have in common: they all utilize the services of a coach. Regardless of how talented or physically superior they may be, each of these athletes contributes great coaching to their success.

As an entrepreneur, it is imperative that you "commit to constant and never-ending improvement" as the great motivational coach Anthony Robbins likes to say.

To do so, you will need to have a coach who challenges you to become the best entrepreneur you can be. The most important job the coach has is to help you see your "blind spots" and provide you with some tools that help you avoid those blind spots and provides you with strategies that keep you motivated and focused on accomplishing your goals.

In business, there is a report called a SWOT analysis. SWOT stands for Strengths, Weaknesses, Opportunities &

Threats. A coach's job is to help you identify these four areas of your life and your business and to make sure you address each area to ensure its success.

So, let's begin a coaching session with a simple exercise. I'd like you to do a personal SWOT report. Take a moment and complete these sentences.

My greatest strengths are_____

My greatest weaknesses are_____

My greatest opportunities are_____

My greatest threats are _____

How did you do? Was it easy to answer the questions? Were you able to complete the exercise? Did you learn anything about yourself while answering the questions?

Unfortunately, there are a lot of people who would not even do the exercise. How about you? Did you do the exercise? If not, why not?

Being an entrepreneur is difficult and challenging yet I can assure you that it can definitely be rewarding and fulfilling. To be successful you must be willing to get out of your comfort zone and do some things that are going to make you uncomfortable. Doing the personal SWOT analysis may make you a little uncomfortable and be difficult to complete, but rest assured you can learn a lot about yourself if you're willing to do it.

Here's why. Let's use basketball as a metaphor.

One of the greatest basketball players of all time is Lebron James. His skill and athleticism are unmatched. His gift is being a basketball player and he excels at his sport. Now try to imagine how he achieved his greatness. He obviously has natural gifts and physical abilities, but he also has one of the most intense and committed work ethics of any athlete. He constantly strives to become better. Just try to imagine how many free throws he's taken in practice over the years. Think about how many jump shots he's taken and how many hours he has spent running up and down a basketball court.

Becoming the great basketball player that he is takes a considerable amount of practice, hard work, determination, patience, perseverance, and commitment. And yet, year in and year out, he continues to get better. The way he does this is by having coaches who help him identify the areas in which he can improve his game. By being willing to look at his strengths, weaknesses, opportunities, and threats he can make adjustments to his game that allows him to continually improve and be the best basketball player he can possibly be.

Now what about you? What do you do that helps you improve your skills as an entrepreneur? How committed are you to becoming the best entrepreneur you can possibly be?

One thing you must be willing to do is your own personal SWOT analysis on a regular basis. As a matter of fact, you should do a SWOT analysis on all areas of your life. You should examine your health, relationships, finances, sense of well-being, and even your spirituality.

In order to improve, you must be able to *identify* the areas in which you need to improve. Put another way, the first step in resolving any problem is to admit that there is one. Having a coach who can support you in identifying the areas in which you can improve is invaluable if you are committed to reaching your full potential as an entrepreneur.

What exactly do I mean by coaching? I simply mean that you are open to learning new things about yourself and you are willing to make an investment in your emotional, intellectual, physical, and spiritual aspect of who you are as a human being.

I believe there are 4 types of coaching.

1. Personal coaching
2. Workshop/Seminar coaching
3. Reading
4. Listening

1. Personal Coaching

A personal coach is someone you hire to help you work on a specific area of your life you would like to improve. If you're struggling with relationships, you can hire a relationship coach. If you're having difficulty with your health, you can hire a fitness coach. If you're struggling with your business, you can hire a business coach. There is a limitless amount of coaches available to you no matter what area of interest you're looking for.

The International Coaching Federation (ICF) defines coaching as "partnering with clients in a thought-provoking and creative process that inspires them to maximize their personal and professional potential."

Coaching is a distinct service and differs greatly from therapy, consulting, mentoring, or training.

In a previous chapter, I talked about the importance of therapy in helping heal and resolve emotional conflict. I will now make a distinction between coaching and therapy. Therapy deals with healing emotional wounds from your past. It is a way of identifying subconscious limiting beliefs you may be holding on to about yourself that may be sabotaging your life in the present. As mentioned in that previous chapter, I believe it is important to make peace with your past and let go of any unresolved emotional conflict or early trauma.

On the other hand, coaching deals with the present moment and the future. It allows you to focus on where you're going versus where you've been. A great coach is someone who will listen to you with an open heart and an open mind and will share insights and wisdom that allows you to come up with your own answers and conclusions about your life. Their job isn't to necessarily provide answers, but to make sure you're asking the right questions in which you then answer for yourself. They are also responsible for being an accountability partner who is committed to your success and is willing to ensure you keep your word and your commitments about the goals and dreams you set for yourself.

In the same way that a basketball coach can't take a shot for you, but they can ensure you have the right technique and form to be the best shooter possible, a coach can't live your life for you but they can provide you with a separate set of eyes that can see things that you may not be able to see. Their job is to bring attention to these things, so you can then choose to change them if needed.

The really good news is there is an infinite number of coaches available to you. As a matter of fact, coaching is one of the fastest-growing industries in the country right now and there are coaches for every niche you might be interested in.

The really bad news is there are countless numbers of coaches who are not effective and some even border on being scam artists, so it's important for you to do your due diligence and take your time finding a coach who is right for you.

If you're thinking about hiring a life coach here are a few questions you should be asking yourself.

Are you coachable?

Truth be told there are some people who are simply not coachable. They refuse to listen to others and they think they know everything. They are arrogant, argumentative, and closed-minded. Needless to say, they would probably never hire a coach. What about you? Are you coachable? Are you open-minded and ready to learn? Since you're reading this book I am going to assume that you are, so if you're coachable, you're ready to become a New Face

Entrepreneur.

What do you want to accomplish if you hire a coach?

It's important for you to recognize if and when you need a coach and what specific goals you want to accomplish. For example, do you want to expand your business? Is your goal to lose weight? Do you want to be better organized? Do you want to make more money? Do you want to locate your soul mate? Be very specific about your goals before you begin looking for a coach because your coach should be chosen based on your specific needs. In other words, if you're looking for a coach to help you make money it's probably not a good idea to hire a health coach. By identifying exactly what your needs are you can then choose a specific coach who can fulfill those needs.

How much are you willing to invest in a coach?

This is a really important question. In most cases "you get what you pay for" applies here. You must be willing to assess your financial situation and decide how much you are willing to invest in yourself to accomplish your goals. Coaching costs vary tremendously across the spectrum so coming up with a realistic amount you can afford is critical. There is no such thing as a 'quick fix' in coaching, so if that is your goal coaching probably isn't right for you. Coaching is a process that takes time and commitment, so understanding this upfront should encourage you to set an amount you're comfortable with and can commit to.

What type of coaching structure will be most effective for you?

Some people prefer face-to-face coaching while others prefer online coaching. Which are you most comfortable with? Are you comfortable using online technology like live video calls, or, are you comfortable with phone calls? Do you need to communicate with your coach once a day, once a week, or once a month? These are a few questions you will have to ask once you start looking for a coach. Once you can answer them, then it will make it easier for you to decide if the coach you choose can meet your needs and provide the structure you're most comfortable with.

Once you can answer these questions you are then ready to seek out a coach. Here are a few questions you should ask your coach before you hire one.

What experience or credentials do they have as a coach?

I do not believe that a coach necessarily has to have a coaching certification to be a great coach. I would, however, begin by asking them if they have certifications for the specific type of coaching you're looking for. The first thing I usually look for is the coach's own level of success. I look for results before I look for credentials. How successful is the coach in their own life? If I'm looking for a relationship coach what type of relationship does that coach currently have? Are they happily married? Are they in a successful relationship? If I'm looking for a financial coach what levels of financial success have they achieved?

The best way to find out how good a coach they are is by reviewing testimonies and referrals. Do not be afraid to ask them to speak to one or more of their clients to get feedback on how well they coach. Don't just go by the testimonies on their websites. Ask to speak to one of their clients so you can get honest feedback on how well they coach. If they are a really good coach they will have no problem allowing you to speak with past clients. Always get referrals before you hire a coach.

Another source of information about a coach is through their social media profiles. Be sure to check their sites on Facebook, Twitter, LinkedIn, and Instagram to get a good feel for that particular coach. Of course, you will want to check out their primary website and blog because their content will tell you a lot about that coach and what their philosophies and values are. Herein lies the key to locating a great coach. Make sure their values and philosophies align with yours. If they do, you've possibly found the right coach.

What are their fees?

Be sure you fully understand their cost and what you're paying for. It's also a good idea to get something in writing that you can verify what is expected from the coach. You should know exactly what you're paying for and what you can expect.

Are the coaching sessions live or online?

Be sure to understand the delivery of the coaching services. Will you meet face-to-face or online? Will there be phone calls or email communications? Is it an online course or is it a well-structured curriculum that you receive by mail?

What is the time commitment required?

Make sure you understand the coaching timeline. Are there 1-hour calls? How often will the coaching sessions be? How many times a week will the sessions be? Will the sessions be recorded, and do you have access to them after the session is over?

These are just a few questions to consider asking a coach. Use them as guidelines as you decide. The most important thing is to trust your own inner wisdom. If you will pay attention to that still small voice within you I'm certain it will guide you to the coach who is perfect for you - so do your homework, ask lots of questions, and be ready to be coached.

2. Workshop/Seminar coaching

My favorite form of coaching is workshops and seminars. I love interacting with others while learning about myself. I have received the most value from engaging in 2-3-day seminars that challenged me to take a really good look at my behaviors and myself and then be willing to change. The advantage of being in a workshop is being with like-minded people who are there to support you in your growth and receiving feedback from those people. Unlike personal coaching, seminar coaching provides you with a lot of different perspectives on how you show up in the world and provides instant feedback.

3. Reading

Reading is one of my favorite past times and it is a great way to coach yourself to become better. There is definitely no shortage of books on the market, so it's up to you to find books that interest you and provide you with information to support you in creating your desired results. Let me also state that *readers become leaders.* Reading is exercise for the brain and I fervently believe you should be working out your brain on a regular basis. Make reading a high priority in your life because it should be.

4. Listening

There are some people who simply do not like to read but that should not keep them from learning. Listening to audiobooks and watching educational videos are great alternatives to reading. One of my favorite forms of listening is Podcasts. Podcasts are like radio shows for the mind. There is an endless number of podcasts covering an infinite number of topics so there is no excuse for not listening and learning as an entrepreneur. I highly recommend you check out my podcast based on this book *The Joy, Passion and Profit Podcast.* Find it at www.joypassionprofit.com. On the podcast, I share tips and strategies supporting entrepreneurs to build companies that change the world. I also interview entrepreneurs who share their insights and wisdom to empower others to grow their businesses while making a positive impact on the world.

In summary, coaching is a lifelong process that you should commit to. Finding the right coach can be instrumental in helping you build your company and making it a huge success. Be sure to incorporate coaching into your business model and make the investment in yourself that allows you to move through your fears and reach your fullest potential.

If you're looking for some resources for coaching be sure to check out these sites:

dreambuilderprogram.com
brendon.com
ebenpagantraining.com
tonyrobbins.com
landmarkworldwide.com
worldworkstrainings.com

"At the end of the day, it's not about what you have or even what you've accomplished... it's about who you've lifted up, who you've made better, it's about what you've given back."

Denzel Washington

Chapter 12

Be In Service

I love this quote from Denzel Washington because it sums up exactly why I do what I do.

> *"At the end of the day, it's not about what you have or even what you've accomplished...it's about who you've lifted up, who you've made better, it's about what you've given back."*

I am a writer because I want to encourage people to be made better. I am a speaker because I want to lift people up to reach their full potential. I am an entrepreneur because I want to give back and support others in waking up to who they really are. I do all these things as a way of being in service to humanity and acknowledging the Infinite Intelligence that created the Universe.

Now that we are at the end of the book I want to share a little secret with you. No matter what you may accomplish and no matter how much money you have made, if you aren't being in service to humanity something will always be missing. It's been said, "what good does it profit a man to gain the whole world if he loses his soul in the process?" Truer words have never been spoken.

So, what exactly does 'being in service' to humanity actually mean?

Simply stated, it means you are sharing your gifts and talents with the world in an effort to make it a better place. This does not mean you have to build a billion-dollar company or impact the lives of millions. It means you are using your God-given talents to be in service to others.

I'm reminded of this quote from Dr. Martin Luther King Jr. "Everybody can be great...because anybody can serve. You don't have to have a college degree to serve. You don't have to make your subject and verb agree to serve. You only need a heart full of grace. A soul generated by love."

"You only need a heart full of grace and a soul generated by love." These words are seldom used in the context of entrepreneurship, but rest assured they apply. No matter what product you produce or what service you provide a soul generated by love will always produce the best results.

You can be a software developer, a real estate investor, a chef, a web designer, a teacher or an entrepreneur. It doesn't matter what profession you're in. If you have a heart full of grace and a soul generated by love you are more likely to succeed.

There is a misconception that most entrepreneurs are heartless greedy automatons who only think of money and profits. Obviously, this may be true in some cases, but I believe the majority of entrepreneurs do not think or feel this way. Unfortunately, throughout our current culture, the focus on financial compensation is what drives too many entrepreneurs to put profits before making a difference, and that is the reason I've written this book.

The subtitle of this book states: "an entrepreneur's guide to joy, passion and profits in business." And that is exactly what I want you to experience, in that particular order. I want you to have joy in your business because if you aren't having fun I can assure you that you're doing business the wrong way. I want you to have passion for your products and services, so you can create the best products and services available. And I definitely want you to have profits, otherwise, you will go out of business.

A sure-fire way to experience joy, passion, and profits is to be in service to humanity. I would like to review the chapters of this book because there is a reason I put together the chapters in the order in which they appear. Each chapter builds on the previous one and they all culminate into this final chapter of being in service, so let's go over them one more time to ensure you have received the full message of becoming a New Face Entrepreneur.

What Is an Entrepreneur?

An entrepreneur is someone who receives compensation in exchange for a product or a service. A New Face Entrepreneur chooses to receive spiritual compensation then emotional compensation and finally financial compensation in exchange for products or services.

Do You Really Have What It Takes to Be an Entrepreneur?

You have everything you need already inside you to be an

entrepreneur. You are blessed with unique gifts and talents and your job is to discover them and share those gifts and talents with the world.

Compassionate Capitalism

Capitalism can be a force for good and money can be used to resolve the majority of challenges facing our world. You can make as much money as you want and the more you make the bigger the difference you can make in the world.

Trust Your Inner Wisdom

Learning to listen to and trust your intuition is your secret weapon to success. Acknowledging your connection to a power greater than yourself is a surefire way to receiving insights and guidance to help you accomplish all your goals.

The Glue That Holds Your Company Together

Relationships are definitely the glue that holds your company together and you make them top priority by building a culture of inclusiveness and diversity. Using sports as a metaphor, you build a winning team by being an amazing coach.

It's Not About the Money

Entrepreneurship can be a source of creative expression that allows you to express your creativity while making a difference in the world by sharing your gifts. By tuning in to the Universal Radio you have an infinite supply of divine ideas to drive your business and create new products and services.

It's All About the Money

Making lots and lots of money is a very good thing when used to better humanity. Being fiscally responsible and sharing your wealth will activate Infinite Intelligence to provide you with more abundance and more opportunities to increase your wealth.

There Is No Such Thing as Failure

There is no such thing as failure - there is only the nonattainment of a desired result. Within every adversity, there is a gift and a lesson designed to help you grow and become the best version of yourself. Embrace "failure" head on and use it to become better. Fail fast, learn faster.

Moonshots & MTPs

Always shoot for the moon because even if you miss you will still be amongst the stars. Don't be afraid to dream big. Understand that you are the master of your destiny and only you can decide what is realistic or not.

Side Hustles and the Solopreneur

There are countless ways to generate additional income. First and foremost, ensure you have the right attitude and mindset about whatever job you may have. If you aren't happy with your current situation, change it. Find a Side Hustle or become a Solopreneur.

The Power of Coaching

Having the right coaches and mentors are essential for your success. Seek out teachers who share your same values and learn from them. Commit to constant and never-ending improvement and make personal development a high priority in your life. Remember, you are a divine manifestation of the Infinite Intelligence that created this Universe and therefore you are divine. Connect with others who support your divinity.

Be in Service

Now we've come full circle and we're back where we started from at the beginning of this chapter. When you combine the lessons you've learned from the previous chapters and made a commitment to be in service to humanity, you have now joined the ranks of a New Face Entrepreneur. You've learned to love and appreciate yourself for the amazing human being that you are. You've discovered your unique gifts and talents and you are now receiving spiritual, emotional, and financial compensation in exchange for your unique products and services. You are serving others by sharing your gifts and talents through your products and services and you are giving back by investing your money, time, and talents to help uplift others.

And last but not least, you are experiencing joy, passion, and profits in your business and you are whole and complete as a New Face Entrepreneur.

I hope this book has instilled a sense of optimism and hope for the future within you. Contrary to mainstream media, I believe the future is filled with infinite possibilities for anyone who is willing to put forth the effort. There has never been a better time to be alive on this planet than right now, and our best days are definitely ahead of us, not behind us.

So, go out there and be a part of the solution. Use your gifts to eradicate a challenge that currently faces our world. Know with absolute certainty that one person can make a difference and choose to be that person. Make a difference in the world and lift up others to do the same.

As you go through life take Dr. King's advice: have a heart full of grace and a soul generated by love and you will change the world.

I'm going to sign off with a writing by a guy named Jesse Elder, jesseelder.com.

Let his words permeate your mind and fill your heart.

I'll see you at the mountaintop!

Take care,
Michael

FACT
If you are not madly in love
with every area of your life,
overflowing in every area
of your life which matters to you,
waking up each day feeling refreshed
and deeply rejuvenated
with a smile on your face
and a song in your heart,
there is a reason for this.

FACT
If you do not feel turned on
by life's richness and rewards,
if you do not feel the pulsing power
of potent natural energy
as it courses like gentle lightning
through your system,
if you do not feel like you are being
deliciously hunted by your desires
which reveal themselves to you at every turn,
if you do not beam love and light
which brightens the fields of those
whom you meet throughout your day,
it is only because you do not understand
the way this universe actually works.

FACT
If you do not experience the grounded thrill
of adventure on a regular basis
and that quiet inner laughter

which always tells you that ALL IS WELL,
it is only because you do not
understand the power of your
seeds - and so you continue to
plant without intention and you call
the painful results "just the price you have to pay".
Love is your natural state.
Love is the base frequency of this reality.
Love is the bond that holds the pieces together.
Love is the force that attracts the components.
NOTHING in your life
is untouched by the seeds you sow.
This is a predictable world.
You live in a VERY CONSISTENT REALITY.
And your PRESENT moment life experiences
are ALWAYS and ONLY the EXACT reflection
of the seeds you have sown.

FACT
There is SO MUCH MORE for you
than you can even fathom.
The limits of your wildest dreams
cannot be reached,
for this universe is expanding even faster
than your mind or even your heart can know.
You will never run out of "good"...
because the GOOD in this world is GROWING.
You will never reach the end of "happy"...
Because there is MORE JOY available to you
than you may ever know.
You will never run out of RESOURCES

because there is always more available for you.
You will never reach the end of REASONS
to feel so good it makes your heart burst
with light and love.
You will never run out of MONEY since money
is ALWAYS flowing to you in EXACT proportion
to your desires and expectations of it.
Can you not see...?
This universe is providing you with the EXACT
requests you have been making.
The seeds you have been sowing.
If you're not madly in love with the
EXACT LIFE you have today...
You are simply not planting the right seeds.
You're the gardener, not the garden.
You are reaping what you sow.
Always and without end.
And if you choose carefully what
to sow... the results will always
surprise and delight you.
Choosing to LIVE the LIFE that thrills you
is easy, fast and incredibly fun.
As the RESULTS show up in DIRECT and PERFECT
proportion to the seeds you sow...
no proof will be greater than the speed
with which your energy and environment
upgrades to reflect your VISION.

FACT
You are already sowing seeds.
You can't NOT.

I get it.
Maybe you have bought the LIES...
The LIE... that LIVING
without your DREAMS is OKAY
The LIE... of "No Pain, No Gain"
The LIE... of "Suffer To Succeed"
The LIE... of "You Are Worthless"
The LIE... of "You Are Not Enough"
The LIE... of "You are UN-LOVABLE"
The LIE... of "I'll be HAPPY, LATER"
Have you not indulged in these long enough?
Don't you know DEEP DOWN that you deserve MORE
and that MORE is available...NOW?
How long will go without feeling
all the POWER that's in your heart?
How long will you go chasing MONEY
instead of letting it chase YOU?
How long will you go sleeping alone
and isolated, feeling disconnected...
When you could be ravished and wrapped up
in the intertwined perfection of delicious ecstasy
with your equal and perfect counterpart?
LIFE IS MEANT TO BE FUN.
LIFE IS NOT SUPPOSED TO BE A STRUGGLE.
LIFE IS A PRECIOUS GIFT.
AND... It's time to unwrap your PRESENCE.
You have everything
inside of you that you require.
Just let it out.

Bio

Coach Michael Taylor is an entrepreneur, author (7 books), motivational speaker, and radio show host who has dedicated his life to empowering men and women to reach their full potential. He knows first-hand how to overcome adversity and build a rewarding and fulfilling life and he is sharing his knowledge and wisdom with others to support them in creating the life of their dreams.

He is no stranger to adversity and challenges. He was born in the inner-city projects of Corpus Christi, Texas, to a single mother with six children. Although he dropped out of high school in the 11th grade, his commitment to living an extraordinary life supported him in defying the odds.

With persistence, patience, and perseverance he was able to climb the corporate ladder of success and become a very successful mid-level manager of a multi-million dollar building supply center at the tender young age of 21. After approximately eight years, he was then faced with another set of challenges as he experienced the pain and humiliation of divorce, bankruptcy, and foreclosure and found himself contemplating suicide.

Bankrupt and alone, he committed to rebuilding his life which propelled him to begin a 25-year inner journey of personal transformation which resulted in him discovering his true self and his passions for living. As a result, he is now happily married (16 years) and living his dream of living an extraordinary life while being in service to others. Through his books, lectures, and radio program, he now coaches others on how to become genuinely happy with their lives and live the lives they were born to live.

coachmichaeltaylor.com
shatterinblackmalestereotypes.com
adversityisyourgreatestally.com
creationpublishing.com
anewconversationwithmen.com
joypassionprofit.com

Contact us
Email: mtaylor@coachmichaeltaylor.com
Phone: 713-303-2067

Resources

If you're looking for inspiration and motivation to help you continue your growth, check out a few of my favorite sites that have contributed to my success.

liveyourmessage.com

ebenpagantraining.com

diamandis.com

tonyrobbins.com

deepakchopra.com

mindvalley.com

motivatingthemasses.com

marymorrissey.com

unity.org

michaelbernardbeckwith.com

thework.com

seatofthesoul.com

nealedonaldwalsch.com

marianne.com

drwaynedyer.com

www.ingramcontent.com/pod-product-compliance
Lightning Source LLC
Chambersburg PA
CBHW060403220326
41598CB00023B/3002